Contents

D1783786

WRITTEN BY : PATRICIA DINGWALL
SERIES DESIGNER AND EDITOR : MALCOLM PARKER
ASSISTANT EDITOR : CAROLINE HILLERY
PRINTED IN ENGLAND
PUBLISHED BY DISCOVERY GUIDES LIMITED,
1 MARKET PLACE, MIDDLETON-IN-TEESDALE,
COUNTY DURHAM, DL12 0QG. TEL & FAX (0833)40638

Discovery Guides Limited wish to thank all those persons, organisations, official bodies and their officers, for their kind assistance in the production of this publication.

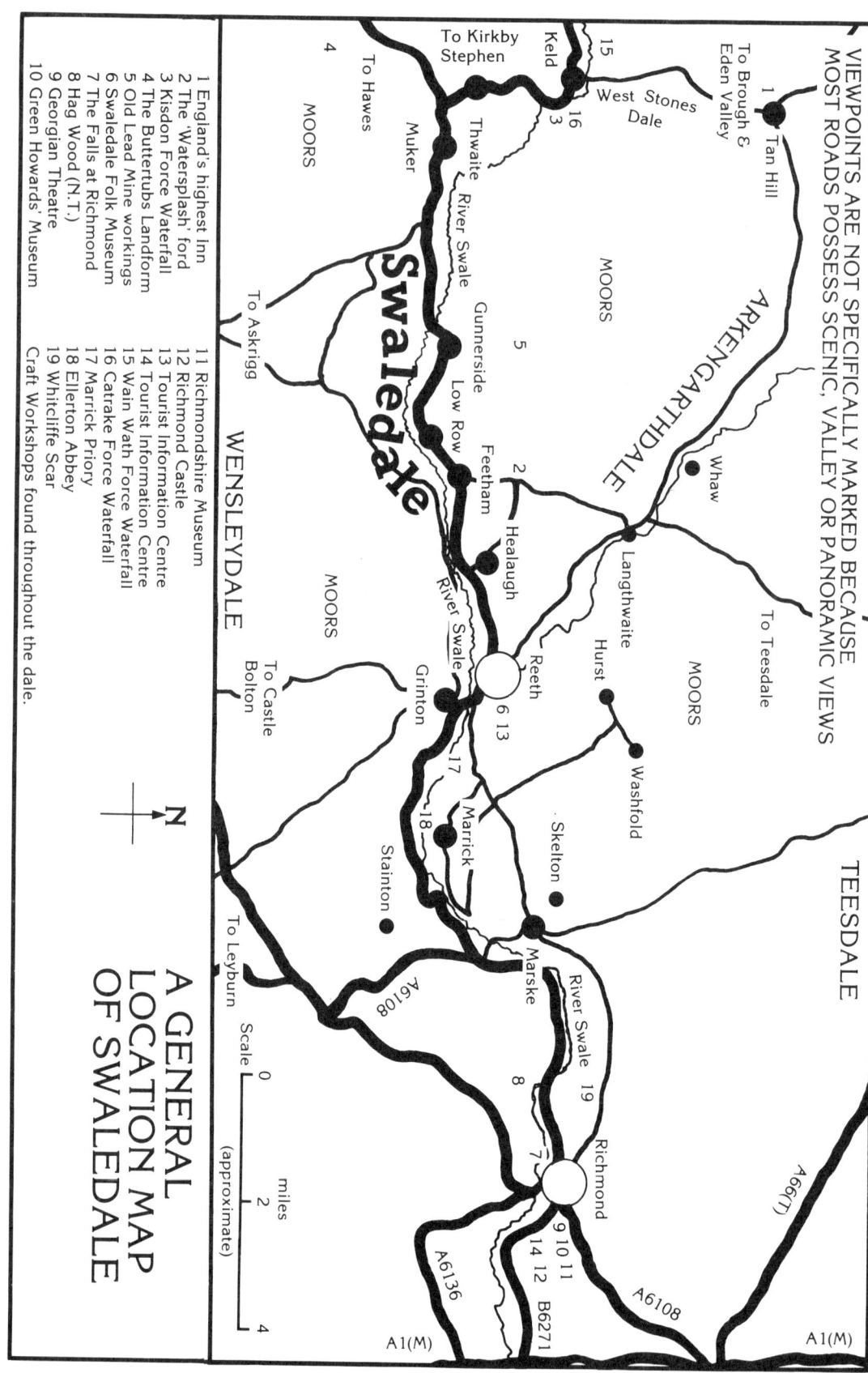

A GENERAL LOCATION MAP OF SWALEDALE

VIEWPOINTS ARE NOT SPECIFICALLY MARKED BECAUSE MOST ROADS POSSESS SCENIC, VALLEY OR PANORAMIC VIEWS

1 England's highest Inn
2 The 'Watersplash' ford
3 Kisdon Force Waterfall
4 The Buttertubs Landform
5 Old Lead Mine workings
6 Swaledale Folk Museum
7 The Falls at Richmond
8 Hag Wood (N.T.)
9 Georgian Theatre
10 Green Howards' Museum
11 Richmondshire Museum
12 Richmond Castle
13 Tourist Information Centre
14 Tourist Information Centre
15 Wain Wath Force Waterfall
16 Catrake Force Waterfall
17 Marrick Priory
18 Ellerton Abbey
19 Whitcliffe Scar

Craft Workshops found throughout the dale.

Scale

0   2   4

miles

(approximate)

N

Introduction

Surrounded by some of the highest fell-tops of the Pennines, Swaledale is a narrow valley where streams hurry down steep hillsides, cascading over many waterfalls, before joining the Swale on its course through the fertile valley floor. Moorland paths stride across wide expanses of heather, purple to the horizon in late summer, where the only sounds may be the whirring wings of a startled grouse or the alarm call of a solitary curlew. On the valley floor of Swaledale and Arkengarthdale the paths wander through meadows in early summer ablaze with the gold of buttercups and beside hedges white with hawthorn, never far from the sight or the sound of water. It is a landscape of stone walls and of houses built and roofed with stone, a place where one can step back in time to such an extent that Swaledale and Arkengarthdale were chosen to provide some of the background to the immensely popular 'Herriot' series on television.

Both Swaledale and Arkengarthdale form part of the Yorkshire Dales National Park. After the last war, people began to realise that, owing to mechanisation and other pressures, the British countryside was changing rapidly, and a traditional landscape was in danger of disappearing. It had long been accepted that a fine building or a stately home should be preserved and that a beautiful garden or a landscape designed by Capability Brown should be maintained for future generations to enjoy. A distinctive landscape made by generations of farmers, with traditional buildings, is of no less value, and it was in recognition of this that in 1950 Parliament passed a bill to approve the creation of National Parks in special areas of the country.

A National Park Authority is not the owner of the land and has no power to coerce people against their will, but by education and by advice on the best methods of conservation helps to preserve the scenery, the wild life and the traditional buildings of its area. It is not part of its duty to promote tourism, and, indeed, very large numbers of tourists may create an extra problem, but the Park Authorities know that the Yorkshire Dales have been popular with holiday makers for many years and they try to ensure that people who come to the area can enjoy it to the full. They provide visitor centres, produce leaflets and conduct guided walks, as well as negotiating access with the owners of popular places, keeping footpaths in repair, making sure there is no litter, and a host of other activities which we may not notice but without which the appearance of the countryside would soon deteriorate. A better understanding of this countryside, and some knowledge of how it came to be, will encourage visitors to recognise its value and assist in its preservation.

The market town of the Dales is Richmond, situated on a rock at the mouth of Swaledale, between the Pennine hills and the Yorkshire plain. This Richmond was the first of all the Richmonds in the world. In 1071 the Norman Alan Rufus chose this place for his great castle, and the Honour of Richmond had been in existence for some 400 years before King Henry VII rebuilt his manor house at Sheen in Surrey and renamed it Richmond to honour the memory of his father, Edmund Tudor, Earl of Richmond.

Richmond is a fascinating place for those interested in history or in architecture. The castle keep still towers above the town, demonstrating the power and skill of the Normans who built it. Not far away is Easby Abbey, now ruined but where the life of the monks can still be traced. Buildings from the 18th century, named the 'Age of Elegance' by Sir Arthur Bryant, are to be seen everywhere in a walk round the town of Richmond, and its Georgian theatre is unique.

A very different way of life can be imagined from the remains of the lead mining activities of former days in Arkengarthdale and Swaledale where huge heaps of debris and deep gullies scarring the hillsides make one wonder at the immense energy of the men who worked here, and at the technological achievements which succeeded in driving miles of tunnels into the hills and extracting and smelting the ore, often with water as their only source of power.

It is possible to stay in an C18th hotel, with all modern comforts added, or in an even older traditional inn. There are guest houses catering for just a few special guests, and friendly bed-and-breakfast in family homes. One can rent a stone-built cottage or choose a modern caravan site with excellent facilities. Whatever the choice, the visitor will find everywhere the warmth of welcome and willingness to be helpful which is characteristic of the people who live in this beautiful part of Yorkshire.

Some visitors arrive thankfully from a long distance walk, others comfortably by car, but whether one's interest is in spectacular scenery, wild flowers or people of past ages, or just in a peaceful holiday in idyllic surroundings, it is easy to fall in love with Swaledale.

BRITISH TELECOM Please note that it is the intention of British Telecom eventually to introduce a uniform six figure telephone number throughout the country, in addition to the code. In the early 1990s an extra numeral may be added to any five figure numbers given here. Information will be given automatically to callers using the old number.

TOURIST INFORMATION CENTRES

RICHMOND
Friary Gardens,
Victoria Road,
Richmond,
North Yorkshire DL10 4AJ
Tel: Richmond (0748) 850252

REETH
Swaledale Folk Museum,
Reeth Green.
Tel: (0748) 84373
(Open from Easter to end October)

SCOTCH CORNER
Rank Motorway Service Area,
Near roundabout, A1M and A66.
Tel: (0325) 377677.
(Open April to October)

YORKSHIRE DALES NATIONAL PARK
National Park Head Office,
Colvend, Hebden Road,
Grassington, Skipton,
North Yorkshire BD23 5LB
Tel: Grassington (0765) 75274

NATIONAL PARK VISITOR CENTRES
There is no centre in Swaledale, but the Visitor Centres at **Aysgarth** and **Hawes** in Wensleydale are within easy reach.

NATIONAL PARK INFORMATION POINTS
These have leaflets of Swaledale Walks etc.
Gunnerside, The Post Office.
Muker, The Village Store and Tea Shop.
Reeth, The Swaledale Folk Museum.

ACCOMMODATION

The visitor has a wide choice of hotels, guest houses and bed-and-breakfast homes, or self-catering accommodation. Some are found on the cover of this guide, but tourist offices can supply lists.
CARAVANS AND CAMPING There are well appointed parks at Brompton on Swale and in the lower Dale to the west of Richmond. Possibilities are limited at the upper end of the Dale, but there is a pleasant farm site near Muker.

YOUTH HOSTELS There are two hostels:
Grinton Tel: (0748) 84206.
Keld Tel: (0748) 86259.

RICHMOND PARKING Disc parking allowing up to two hours operates in Richmond town centre, including the market place. Discs are available free from the Tourist Information Centre and from local shops. For longer times, there are a number of off-street car parks within walking distance of the town centre.
Market days: Outdoor, Saturday: Mini-indoor, Thursday: Early closing, Wednesday.

BUS SERVICES There is a regular daily bus service between Richmond and Darlington and eslsewhere. There is an infrequent service on weekdays between Richmond, Reeth, Gunnerside and Keld. For information, contact: United Automobile Services, Grange Road, Darlington, Co. Durham. Tel: (0325) 468771
BRITISH RAIL There is no railway to Richmond. United Automobile Services buses run from Darlington. For British Rail enquiries, contact Darlington Tel: (0325) 355111

MAPS The Ordnance Survey Outdoor Leisure Map number 30, 'Yorkshire Dales Northern and Central Areas' 1:25,000 (4cm to 1km, 2.5in to 1 mile) shows footpaths and other details very clearly. It includes Swaledale and Arkengarthdale but stops just short of Richmond. To include both dales and Richmond on the Ordnance Survey 1:50 000 Series, it is necessary to have number 92 (which has Richmond inconveniently sited in the extreme south-east corner) and numbers 98 and 99. The Tourist Map, 'The Yorkshire Dales', published by Estate Publications is a useful map for motorists, with historic sites, camp sites, etc. marked in red.

SPORTS FACILITIES
Fishing The Tourist Information Office can supply a list of fishing which may be available to visitors, with information about the necessary permits and rod licences.
Richmond Bowls Club, Ronaldshay Park, Richmond. Woods, etc. are available for visitors.
Richmond Golf Club, New Club House, Bend Hagg, Richmond. Visitors are welcome.
Richmondshire Swimming Pool, Old Station Yard, Richmond. Modern indoor pool, open daily after midday, times varying slightly.

TOILETS Public toilets in the Dales are available in the following villages: Gunnerside, Keld, Langthwaite, Muker, Reeth.

WEATHERLINE Tel: (0898) 500417

The Rocks that Made Swaledale

"Whereas there have been found in the tops of these mountains.... stones like sea winkles or cockles and other sea fish ....I deeme them to be the undoubted tokens of the generall deluge that surrounde the face of the whole earth in Noah's time". Camden, describing Richmondshire in 1636, may have been mistaken about the extent of Noah's flood but he was correct in deducing that the land had been formed under the sea.

Millions of years ago, during the geological Carboniferous period, the land which is now Britain lay close to the equator under tropical seas. These seas teemed with small creatures and their shells of calcium carbonate drifted down to form thick limestone sediments. Then rivers carrying detritus from a northern land-mass pushed into the seas and deposited firstly fine mud and silt on top of the limestone and then sand upon sand until a great delta gradually built up. Here swamps and vegetation formed. Then the sea flooded in again and the cycle of deposition began once more.

This happened many times as sea and rivers in turn laid down the layers of limestones, shales and sandstones known today as the Yoredale Series (from the river Ure in Wensleydale) until the steady uplift of the underlying rock mass, the Askrigg block, raised the land clear of the sea. The topmost layer laid down millions of years ago over the Yoredale Series was a coarse erosion-resistant sandstone known to us as Millstone Grit and this rock caps the hills around Swaledale, giving them comparatively rounded tops in contrast to the steep slopes of the Dale. Millstone Grit is a durable rock which becomes overlain with waterlogged soil and peat.

In the valley itself water and ice cut down through the layers of limestone, shale and sandstone. The softer shales washed down into gentle slopes while the harder rocks, more resistant to weathering, formed the 'scars' and 'edges' which are so prominent a feature. Fremington Edge which dominates the lower part of the Dale and Cotterby Scar, alongside the road near Keld, are examples of thick beds of limestone.

This combination of hard rock alternating with shale makes the fine waterfalls, and here the layering of the rocks can be appreciated. As the underlying weak shale becomes eroded away by the river, the harder rock on top of it becomes undercut and eventually a piece breaks off and is washed downstream, forming the characteristic stepped waterfalls, very evident in places like Wainwath Force and many other falls, including the falls at Richmond where the layers of rock are clearly seen. Flagstones and roofing slates come from very thinly layered beds of sandstone.

A fascinating geological formation is seen at the Buttertubs, by the road between Muker and Hawes. Limestone is soluble and rainwater acidified just by carbon dioxide in the atmosphere can affect it. At the Buttertubs the result of water solution can be seen in the formation of deep chasms, pot-holes and vertical columns with slightly fluted sides.

The decaying swamps and vegetation formed in the deltas of the Carboniferous period were buried under later sands and the weight of these overlying rocks eventually compressed the mass into coal. Seams of coal in Swaledale are thin but have been exploited in many small diggings on high ground, particuarly around Tan Hill where the seam was over 1 metre thick.

After the limestone beds had been laid down, movements of the earth's crust caused them to fracture and crack. Solutions of minerals from deep within the earth forced their way into vertical fissures and eventually crystallised into minerals, including galena, fluorspar and barytes. The many spoil heaps, hushes and old workings which litter parts of both Swaledale and Arkengarthdale show how eagerly man has searched for the galena, lead ore, at one time the source of the Dales' great industry.

During the Ice Ages the movements of glaciers flowing down Swaledale smoothed the hill tops and widened the valley, and as they melted left behind a debris of rock and clay. The river which had formerly flowed in a channel to the west of Kisdon Hill found its usual course blocked and cut, instead, the deep gorge on the eastern side, isolating the hill which now forms so remarkable a feature. At Richmond also the river cut a new, deep channel, diverted from its original course by a pile of boulder clay. In the valley the ice left a series of moraines, lines of debris, behind which the water gathered into lakes where clay, sand and gravel gradually accumulated. These old lakes and marshes have formed the level ground where the river takes a winding course through fertile alluvial meadows.

The steep side of the Dale makes the Swale one of the swiftest rivers in England, still sweeping debris downstream and on the low-lying ground near Reeth can be seen deposits of gravel only laid down in recent years.

From Iron Age Celts to Anglian Farmers

It is not possible to say when man first came to Swaledale but a few tools dating from neolithic times, more than 2000 BC, have been found in the Dale. There is more evidence of Bronze Age man, including the impressive Maiden Castle. This is a circle, over 70 metres across, cut into the hillside and surrounded by a rampart and outer ditch, with an avenue of stones leading to it. Whether it was built for defence or simply for domestic purposes is not certain, but it is clear from its impressive size that the people who constructed it must have been part of a large and well-organised community. On the south side of the river not far from Grinton, it is only just visible from the road but a footpath passes by it.

Between 300 and 400 BC the Iron Age Celtic people arrived in Britain from Europe and gradually spread throughout the country; their descendants, the Brigantes, being still in occupation of Swaledale when the Romans arrived. These Iron Age people have left evidence of small hut settlements and fields in parts of the dale and they may have continued to make use of some Bronze Age sites.

Swaledale is particularly rich in pre-historic remains and much work has yet to be done by archaeologists, but even the least expert visitor can see a massive earth embankment built across the Dale just to the west of Grinton and continuing on the other side of the river up to Fremington Edge. The ground immediately beside the river was probably a marsh when this was built. Further to the west, across the river from Reeth, is another embankment and ditch in a similar direction.

It was not until the first century AD that the Romans, having subdued the South of England, began to move against the northern tribes. In 69 AD Venutius, as leader of the Brigantian tribes, organised the construction of huge defences at Stanwick, north of Richmond. In spite of this the Brigantian tribes were defeated in 79 AD and Roman power gradually consolidated in the North of England. The Roman governor Agricola established a fort at Cataractonium and a civilian settlement in association with it grew into a considerable town. No evidence has been found of Roman settlement in Swaledale which was probably thinly populated and giving no trouble. The Romans, however, had many uses for lead and they may have been exploiting some of the lead deposits. There is a tradition that they were mining lead at Hurst but no concrete evidence of this can be produced.

As the Romans withdrew from Britain, the Angles and Saxons came from across the North Sea. The first piratical raids were followed by settlers who gradually drove their way further and further west, reaching York about 500 AD but probably not penetrating into Swaledale until some hundred years later. After they had settled in this country, they were converted to Christianity and it is recorded that the Swale was "a river reputed very sacred" because in it Paulinus "baptized with festivall joy above tenne thousand men, besides women and children" in one day.

In their homelands the Anglians had been accustomed to arable farming and after their arrival the pattern of villages and fields which we see today started to take shape. They began to clear the marshy ground by the river to make meadows, and on the well-drained slopes a series of long grassy terraces, still visible in the fields just west of Reeth, probably date from this time, and other such terraces are found near Downholme. These are lynchets, the old ploughed strips of a communally shared field system. Using a heavy plough drawn by a team of several oxen, it was much easier to plough on level ground than on a steep slope, so groups of terraces one above another were constructed. These had the added advantage of preventing the ploughed soil being washed down the slope in wet weather. Strips were still being worked as late as the 16th century.

By the 9th century the Norsemen had invaded Ireland and set up a capital at Dublin. From there they colonised the western part of Cumbria and eventually crossed the Pennines and established their kingdom at York. Their presence in Swaledale is very definite from the persistence of Norse place-names. Gill, Beck and Force are all Norse words, as are names like Thwaite, a clearing in woodland, and Muker, a narrow field (mior akr), and Gunnerside, a shieling or pasture (Gunnar's saetr). The suffix 'ton' on the other hand, denotes an Anglian, or Old English, derivation meaning homestead, as in Fremington, homestead of Fremi's people, or Grinton, green homestead, while the name Reeth is the Old English word for stream.

The Norse settlers came originally from the steep valleys of Western Scandinavia and pursued a traditional pastoral farming, moving animals between winter and summer pastures. Needing large tracts of land for sheep, they lived in isolated farms or scattered settlements on high ground, interfering little with the Anglians in their villages and fields.

Eric Bloodaxe, the last of the Norse rulers, was killed at Stainmore in 954 and Yorkshire became part of the English king's realm until the arrival in 1066 of William the Conqueror. A mixture of Anglians, Danes and Norsemen, and close to the Scottish border, the North of England had little affinity with the South and in 1069 they rose in rebellion against the Normans. William took a terrible revenge. After taking York, he embarked on a deliberate campaign of destruction, in which thousands of people were killed and more starved to death after their homes, crops, food and cattle had been burnt. 'The Harrying of the North' as it became known stretched from York to Durham and as late as 1086 the Domesday Book recorded the majority of places in the North Riding of Yorkshire as 'waste' or 'partly waste'.

To consolidate his position, William established Norman overlords who could dominate the countryside from their huge castles. To Alan Rufus of Brittany, who had fought alongside him at Hastings, he gave the Honour of Richmond, some 440 manors throughout England including a vast estate in Yorkshire. It was Alan Rufus who chose the impregnable site on a rock above the Swale and built a fortress of such size and strength, to protect his Breton followers and to establish his power over the local English.

Most castles of this date were defensive positions built of earth ramparts and wood. Alan built his of stone, and Richmond was the first castle to have its curtain walls strengthened with protective towers. Another exceptional building is Scolland's Hall (named after a steward), the earliest example of such a castle hall with its two storeys and grand chamber. The great keep which still dominates the town was added in the next century by Earl Conan, Alan Rufus's great-nephew. A visitor to Richmond Castle will be impressed by the massive strength and solidity of a medieval fortress and children, in particular, usually enjoy it greatly.

To ensure that any attackers would have no possible cover, a large open space was left outside the castle wall and this 'outer bailey' has since become the market place. The Normans deliberately planned the town and a number of long narrow burgage plots for dwellings were laid out around this space. Settlers, called burgesses, were attracted by promises of protection, freedom from feudal dues and by favourable tenancies. Craftsmen and traders were particularly welcome, to provide for the needs of the castle and the growing community. A market was established and stalls set up. The burgesses also had rights in a large extent of land, fields and pasture, outside the town and these agricultural holdings remained in their possession for many centuries, so that trade and part-time farming were often combined. In time the burgesses acquired the right to regulate life in the town and eventually came to govern it, themselves enjoying many liberties and privileges.

The Dales were left thinly populated after William's cruelties and a large amount of land was reserved by the Normans for 'forest''. This term did not mean that it was all trees in our modern sense. The Normans were passionate lovers of hunting and Forests were extensive tracts of countryside where game, especially deer, were encouraged to breed and where the inhabitants lived under special laws, with the clearing of land, the cutting of wood, the grazing of animals and the keeping of dogs being severely controlled and where all game was reserved for the lord's hunting. In 1100 Count Alan put Robert Arkhil in charge of part of this countryside and it is from him that Arkle Town, Arkle Beck and Arkengarthdale get their names.

The Forest lands of Arkengarthdale and the New Forest, as it was called, and of Upper Swaledale had a small population in isolated holdings and the inhabitants were only permitted to keep a limited number of cattle or pigs on restricted pastures. Sometimes dogs, tied up by the day, were allowed to be loose at night to keep off wolves, for the Forest was full of all kinds of animals as well as game.

In the lower part of Swaledale where the Anglians had already established villages and a system of common fields, life was very different. The people here lived for the most part in small close-knit villages, each man having so many strips on the large open arable fields and meadows, and the right to pasture his animals on the extensive common ground.

The population of the Dale recovered sufficiently to warrant the building of a stone church, and the church of St. Andrew at Grinton is a Norman foundation, though its present exterior dates mainly from later centuries, the western end of the nave and the font being some of the original Norman work. There was no church in the thinly populated Forest area and for many years all corpses had to be carried in wicker coffins to Grinton. The well-defined Corpse Way leading from the upper end of the Dale can be followed by walkers.

Monks, Nuns and Friars

The oldest monastic order of the Western Church was founded in 528 by St. Benedict. Benedictine monks vowed to retire from the world, renounce possessions, live frugally and without women, do manual work, be obedient to the abbot and celebrate Mass daily. St. Augustine, who brought Christianity to Britain, had formerly been a Benedictine monk. Later Augustinian monks took vows of poverty, chastity and obedience, but they were not required to retire from the world and they cared for the spiritual needs of lay people as part of their duty.

Coinciding with Norman rule in England, a surge of religious enthusiasm swept Europe. Monks had grown lax in many of their observances and St. Bernard of Clairvaux determined to revive the primitive simplicity of the original Benedictines. His Cistercian (from Citeaux in France) monks were enjoined to follow Benedict's rule to the dot, to live in remote places and to labour in the fields. So eloquent was Bernard's preaching that women tried to keep away their men-folk lest they should all abandon the world for the cloister.

New monasteries were built in many places. Although a monk had to renounce personal possessions, this did not apply to the monastery as a whole and gifts began to pour in from devout people. Thanks for success, repentance for sins, requests for Masses to be said, all these and many more brought great wealth to the monasteries. Walter de Gaunt had founded a Priory for Augustinian monks at Bridlington and his wife gave these monks the right to collect tithes from Grinton, to make hay and pasture animals. The Cistercians of Rievaulx obtained property in Upper Swaledale with the right to build dwellings for their workers and to enclose land. Some holdings of land in Swaledale were acquired also by Jervaulx Abbey, Coverham Abbey and Easby Abbey.

The monks became expert farmers, doing much to revitalize the country devastated by William, and the Cistercians transformed remote fells and marshes into productive sheep runs. To assist them to clear land, drain marshes and labour in the fields of these vast estates, monasteries employed 'lay brethren', so that in time the work of the monks themselves became that of overseers and administrators. An abbot or prior could be just as grasping as any ordinary secular owner and Swaledale's history records many disputes between local inhabitants and these distant landlords, particularly over the enclosure of land, which deprived the villagers of their communal open pastures.

In 1151 Roald, Constable in charge of Richmond Castle, founded a Premonstratensian Abbey at Easby. This unwieldy name comes from two French words, 'pre' (a meadow) and 'montre' (shown), for the Virgin Mary herself, appearing in a vision, had pointed out the field in France where she wanted the original foundation built. These monks were a branch of the Augustinian order, so they preached, baptized, buried the dead and gave pastoral care to the local people in addition to their monastic duties. In time, they too became wealthy, owning land in a number of places, and the people of Richmond complained about the abbot enclosing a large sheepfold on common ground. An interesting visit may be made to the extensive Abbey ruins.

Marrick Priory was a Benedictine foundation for women, started about 1154. The nuns, who wore black habits, employed lay sisters to do work considered unbecoming for themselves. Nunneries were convenient places for unmarried or elderly relatives, or even discarded mistresses, and discipline was often easy. The rule at Marrick, however, was strict, with outside visiting severely restricted and the entry of novices controlled by the archbishop. The restored Priory is now private but the 365 steps climbing the hill to Marrick village can still be seen.

Across the river stood Ellerton Priory, of which only a ruined tower and remnants of the nave remain. These are on private ground. Only five nuns, wearing the white habits of the Cistercians lived here in 1381 and it was one of the smallest and poorest houses in England.

Determined to live as Christ had done, St. Francis of Assisi gave away all his possessions, living only on what he could beg. Following his example came the mendicant friars, taking vows of total poverty. Friars did not shut themselves into remote monasteries but worked in the towns, amongst the growing population, preaching, hearing confession and visiting. Unfortunately, it was all too easy for a friar to become little more than a pseudo-religious beggar and many acquired dubious reputations, as a song of 1380 warns, "For when the goodman is from hame, And the friar comes to our dame, He spares neither for sin nor shame, But that he does his will". The Franciscan friars, known as Grey Friars from their drab habits, were given land just outside Richmond. A narrow alley, Friar's Wynd and a small arched gateway still exist today. They too received gifts from devout people and their ruined but still beautiful Greyfriars Tower shows that they too accumulated wealth.

Prosperity and Disaster

For some two hundred years after the Norman invasion Richmond grew in prosperity. Protected by its huge castle, with the corn-growing lowlands of the Yorkshire plain on one side and the wool-producing Pennines on the other, it was a natural centre for trade.

By the C13th England's trade was flourishing. In a good year the wool from eight million fleeces would leave English ports for the continent. And it was not only wool; "From England", records a writer in Bruges about 1200, "come wool, hides, lead, tin, coal and cheese". Back came wine, oil, fruit, spices, furs and other luxuries. The burgesses of Richmond levied tolls on the goods sold in the market, and the long lists of these cover all kinds of necessities and luxuries, from corn and wood to olive oil and figs. Some people paid dues to their overlord (often paid in kind) in quantities of imported ginger and pepper, an extremely costly item.

Then in 1314 Robert the Bruce defeated the English king at the battle of Bannockburn and a Scottish army was able to lay waste the countryside as far south as Richmond, though the Scots avoided the easily defended castle. From then on Scottish raids for booty and plunder were a frequent hazard. The burgesses of Richmond, under the great castle, were able to buy off the Scots with large sums of money, very acceptable to the raiders as the easiest form of plunder to carry away, but Swaledale suffered frequent looting. Religious houses were easy targets, Marrick being completely despoiled in 1318 and Ellerton in 1347.

Nor was this their only trouble, for a disastrous summer in 1314 had ruined the hay and corn crops. With many people always living near subsistence level, starvation and disease followed. Hunger and perpetual rain reduced flocks of sheep by two-thirds and a murrain, or disease, of cattle almost wiped out many herds, not only the cows and calves but also the oxen that worked the fields.

But even these disasters were slight compared to the Black Death, bubonic plague, which made its first devastating appearance in England in 1349. Everywhere plague drastically reduced the population. The value of land in Swaledale fell by half, and the desperate shortage of men to work the fields led to the monasteries letting many of their more distant properties. Records in Richmond tell of houses waste and desolate and the town fields uncultivated and overgrown. It was to be a hundred years before the value of land began to rise again.

By the late C15th the religious enthusiasm which had built the monasteries had waned. Friars and monks could be seen enjoying lives of wealth and ease. Many people were ready for the Reformation, seized on by Henry VIII to get rid of the authority of the Pope who was opposing his marriage plans. The Act for the Suppression of the Monasteries meant the closure of Easby Abbey and Ellerton Priory in 1536 and of Marrick and the Grey Friars in 1539. The extensive monastery lands were seized by the Crown and sold to new owners.

The pace of change and the sweeping away of old customs was too swift, and in October 1536 the people in the North rose in support of the old religion. The Pilgrimage of Grace was eagerly followed by a mass of ordinary folk, two of the leaders being Sir Francis Bigod who owned the manor of Healaugh and Anthony Peacock of Arkengarthdate. With muddled and ineffective leadership the rising was easily suppressed by Henry VIII and by the following February Bigod had been captured and the Pilgrimage of Grace was at an end. Bigod and Peacock were executed.

100 men from Richmond and 40 from Swaledale joined another rebellion in 1569, an attempt to depose Elizabeth and restore Catholicism. With no general support it collapsed quickly. The furious queen demanded 700 executions but the more lenient Earl of Sussex was purposely vague about the number actually carried out. Only four men from Richmond and none from Swaledale were executed.

Less than 100 years later came the Civil War. Richmond favoured the king's cause and a regiment of men led by Malger Norton of St. Nicholas fought alongside Prince Rupert at the battle of Marston Moor. After this defeat the town had to suffer the indignity of being occupied by the Scots under David Leslie.

Recurrent outbreaks of plague added to the miseries of the population. In a particularly virulent attack in 1597 and '98 Richmond lost two-thirds of its inhabitants and outbreaks continued throughout the C17th. The town of Wensley, in the neighbouring dale, never recovered its importance after one epidemic. By the middle of the C15th the burgesses of Richmond were collecting from their market tolls less than one quarter of what they had been getting in the C13th, and even as late as 1698, when Celia Fiennes visited the town, she wrote, "I must say it looks like a sad shatter'd town and fallen much to decay and like a disregarded place."

Knitters and Drovers

In spite of the disastrous years the Dales had two invaluable commodities, wool and lead. In Swaledale in the Middle Ages, the monks had transformed empty wastes into vast sheep runs. Secular landlords followed their example and merchants collected wool even from small farms and humble villagers. The Bishop Blaize Inn in Richmond used to be a centre of the trade. Bishop Blaize was so saintly that he could sit safely amongst lions, tigers and bears. Suspected in consequence of being a wizard, he was tortured with the iron combs used for carding wool, thus becoming eminently suitable as the patron saint of wool-combers and wool-merchants.

At first wool was exported raw but over the years the kings of England made deliberate efforts to establish an English cloth trade, even at times prohibiting the export of raw wool and going to great lengths to promote spinning, weaving and knitting. In 1571 a statute ordered that all caps worn on Sundays and holidays had to be knitted, and an act of Charles II required all shrouds to be woollen. Adam Barker was fined £5, then a huge sum, for having his daughter Ann buried in the traditional linen. Her tomb is in Grinton church.

In the days when men wore breeches and hose, there was a great demand for knitted stockings and Richmond was a centre for this trade, "ther is made every fortnight 14 or 16 packes, and every packe contayneth 40 dossen pare". One trader's stock in 1672 included 265 dozen pairs of men's stockings, 118 dozen women's and 92 dozen boys', and it is no wonder that when Defoe visited the town he reported, "Here you see all the people, great and small, a knitting". Everyone, the housewife at her door, the shepherd looking after sheep, people walking to work, even miners in spare moments, knitted to earn a few extra pence. Steam-powered frames for knitting and the advent of long trousers in men's fashions eventually killed the earlier hand-knitting trade, but knitting is carried on today in Swaledale and visitors to Muker will find an age-old tradition in a modern form.

Visitors using the minor road from Arkengarthdale to Low Row may not be aware that they are following in the wake of thousands and thousands of cattle, for this was once part of a great drove road. Cattle could be bred extensively in the Scottish Highlands but the demand for meat was in England. With no refrigeration to preserve carcasses and no railway for transport, animals had to get to their destination alive and on foot.

One of the great cattle fairs was at Crieff, just south of the Highlands. There dealers purchased the cattle and these were then driven south to be sold to the farmers in the grass-lands and dales of Northern England where they could be fattened before being sent on to feed the industrial towns. A herd of 40 or 50 would be put into the charge of a drover, who would have a lad and a couple of dogs to assist him. The cattle were driven about 12 miles a day by the most direct route possible. The drovers avoided towns and cultivated areas and crossed moorland, round the shoulders of hills and over fords. One route came through the Border hills, up the valley of the South Tyne, across Teesdale, over the river Greta to Sleightholme (the Pennine Way follows this part) and from there into Arkengarthdale by Dale Head. The track continued down the Dale to Eskeleth where there was a ford and then crossed moorland to Feetham. It continued up Whitaside Moor into Wensleydale and Wharfedale and eventually to a great fair at Malham Moor.

In the mid-C18th 100,000 cattle were sold each year at Crieff. Similar fairs were held at Dumfries and Falkirk. The drovers, passing along the same routes regularly, became a fraternity with favourite stopping places, the equivalent of the long-distance lorry drivers of today, and this regular traffic of thousands of hooves made wide tracks over the moorland. Some of these later became roads, some remain as footpaths or wide 'green roads' perfect for the walkers of today.

With the wool trade and lead-mining, the Dales were full of people coming and going and many tracks were made by pack-horses, for carts were impractical with no good roads. Laden pack-horses went slowly so the shortest feasible route would be taken and trails would mount steep slopes. The uphill road from Reeth to Marske and Richmond was once a pack-horse trail, and the steeply humped bridge at Ivelet was built in 1698 with pack-horses, not cars, in mind.

Tan Hill Inn was at a meeting place of four such trails and in the past this lonely inn was crowded with travellers, drovers, horse dealers and peddlers, as well as with local miners. Tan Hill is on a seam of coal and although this was only just over a metre thick it was exploited in a number of small mines and underground workings. The coal was sold over a wide area which included Cumbria and Durham. There are many old shafts around Tan Hill and it is unwise for walkers to wander off the footpaths.

Mining for Lead

Spoil heaps, hushes, mine entrances, ruined buildings, gigantic flues, all remains of the lead mining industry, litter parts of Swaledale and Arkengarthdale. The underlying rock is limestone, a sedimentary rock, and past movements of the earth's crust have caused it to fracture, both vertically and horizontally. It is into these cracks, usually the vertical, that minerals, including galena (lead ore), have intruded.

The abbeys and castles of Medieval England were roofed with lead and their gutters, pipes and basins made of it. Lead was exported and many of the great French buildings also were roofed with English lead. In 1091 the bishop of Coutances sent to England for Brismet the plumber to repair the roof of the cathedral which had been struck by lightning. (The Latin for lead is Plumbum, and plumbers were originally workers in lead.) 241 cartloads of lead sent from York to Rouen would have come from the Pennines, although the exact extent of medieval diggings in Swaledale is unknown.

"The men of Sualdale be much usid in digging Leade Owre", wrote Leland in the C16th and it was in the 17th that Dr John Bathurst, Cromwell's physician, bought Arkengarthdale and his son Charles began to develop the mines there. The C.B. hotel in Arkengarthdale still carries the initials of the Bathurst family. In the 18th and 19th centuries new methods of mining and smelting created a huge industry with a thriving population in both Dales.

One of the earliest methods of mining was to dig a shaft down to a vein and then extract the ore. The miners worked along the vein and as one shaft became too difficult to continue, it would be abandoned and another sunk nearby. In places the remains of a row of former shafts are found. Some have collapsed into waterlogged holes and others are very dangerous and have been fenced off to protect livestock.

Visitors may notice what appear at first sight to be natural fissures in the slopes of some hills, but these are, in fact, often man-made 'hushes' from former mining operations. Large areas of such workings are to be seen near Gunnerside and a steep rocky gully near the road from Langthwaite to Low Row is Turf Moor Hush. One method of mining was to construct a dam on the hillside at the top of a vein and collect as much water as possible into it. Using picks, the miners loosened the ground below the dam. They then released the water so that the sudden torrent would sweep down, or 'hush', the earth and rock, and the ore could be more easily extracted. A good vein could be worked in this way time and time again, eventually making a deep gully in the hillside.

Improved technology brought a new method of extraction. Horizontal tunnels, known as levels or adits, could be driven into the steep hillside. These had several advantages as well as enabling deeper veins to be reached. They could provide drainage and they also established a circulation of air, for lack of both had been a great problem in earlier shafts. Rails could be laid in them and the ore brought out in tubs drawn by ponies. Levels were, in fact, driven at a very slight slope so that the water would drain and the tubs run easily toward the exit. The ponies were always small and to protect their heads from the low roof wore leather skull caps, one of which can be seen in the Folk Museum at Reeth. Stone-arched entrances to these adits are still visible and the rail tracks inside could be extensive, Faggergill Mine, for instance, having 25 miles of underground railway.

When the ore, still mixed with other minerals and rock, and at this stage known as 'bouse', had been brought out it was taken to a level dressing floor. Here women and boys used hammers, 'buckers', to crack the rock and separate out the galena from the 'deads', as the rubbish was called, and to crush the ore to a fine gravel. As technology developed in the 19th century, huge water wheels were constructed to drive machinery for this crushing process. Lead ore could be separated from other materials by the use of water in which the rubbish could be washed away while the heavier ore sank to the bottom and could be recovered, and over the years a variety of sieves and 'buddles' were developed for this process.

The dressed ore then had to be taken to a smelt mill. These were sited near streams, so that water-power could be used to drive a wheel which operated a large bellows for the furnace, fired by peat from the moorland. Later, long flues were built which increased the draught to the furnace and also condensed the smoke as it passed along, as well as carrying the highly toxic fumes from the smelting process well away onto waste ground. One of these smelt mills was near Surrender Bridge where the chimney and the flue going up the hillside can cearly be seen. Further up the stream is Old Gang smelt mill which has the remains of the old hearth. At intervals boys were sent up the flues to scrape down the soot from which lead could still be recovered.

At one time there were 20 such mills in the area and the remains of others still exist, sited at the top of Gunnerside Gill, in Swinnergill and on high ground above Grinton.

Spoil heaps, mounds of rubbish from which the lead had been extracted, litter the ground together with the remains of other buildings essential for mining operations. On the hillside above Old Gang smelt mill can be seen the peat store which once held three years' supply of fuel. On private land in Arkengarthdale near the Stang road is a small hexagonal powder house, for gunpowder, used for blasting the rock, had to be stored well away from other buildings. In fact, this was considered too close to people's houses and little used. A forge for the repair of machinery, rails and wagons was always a necessity and buildings now a petrol station near Reeth bridge once provided offices, stables, a saw mill and store rooms for the A.D. Mining Company. Lead was transported by pack-horse and their trails leading from mine and smelt mill provide many footpaths for walkers of today.

In early days miners had worked in small independent groups but by the later part of the C17th, when the owners of the land had seen the profits to be made, larger companies were formed who owned or leased the mineral rights. These could afford to put much more money into the construction of levels and machinery than could the independent miner. The miners were not direct employees of the company but formed their own partnerships of 6 or 8 men and each team would make their own 'bargain' with the company to work a certain section of vein. They were paid according to the amount of dressed lead ore they produced, and this is the reason for the long rows of open bays at the Sir Francis and Bunting mines in Gunnerside, where each 'bouse-stead' held the ore dug by one partnership, so that their earnings could be worked out. Similar 'bargains' were made to drive a length of tunnel or other necessary work. If such a bargain was to prove profitable, the men concerned had to make a good judgement of the conditions and difficulties they might encounter, and miners had to be men of intelligence and independence.

Many of the farms in Swaledale were small and farmers could add to a meagre income by working in the mines. Wages fluctuated with the demand for lead and the outcome of a 'bargain' could never be a certainty, so those miners who had not inherited land acquired, if possible, a small amount of ground on which they could grow a few crops and perhaps keep a cow or a few sheep. The miner had to work in damp mines with dust and poor ventilation, and this combination with some farming was beneficial to health as well as providing something to fall back on in times of hardship. Small fields found on the edge of moorland are often 'intakes' by miners.

The industry brought a vast increase in population. In Arkengarthdale and in Swaledale, from Grinton westwards, the population at the 1801 census was 5,740, but by 1821, the next census, it was 7,480, an addition of 1,740 people, a rise of 30% in 20 years. Many small two storey houses, often in terraces or pairs, were built in Arkengarthdale and at Low Row, Feetham, Gunnerside and other villages, as well as cottages on the higher ground, of which only foundations remain. It is hard to imagine today that the hamlet of Booze once had 41 houses and that both Dales were a hive of industry.

By the middle of the C19th Britain, once the leading producer of lead, had slipped behind other countries. South America, able to extract silver from its lead ore, could sell the residue cheaply. The price of lead fell. In addition, the good veins of ore in Swaledale were worked out. The Blakethwaite Company gave up in 1866 and the Old Gang Company went into liquidation in 1906. Arkengarthdale's mines produced good profits for a while but even here the mines were abandoned in 1912. Many people left for the industrial towns or emigrated. By 1901 the population had fallen from 7,480 to 2,520. In 1971 it was only 1644. In Healaugh in 1851 there were 112 children under 14, in 1972 there were none.

Today the National Park has reached agreements with the owners which will enable some old mine buildings to be preserved. Visitors will find particular interest in a walk up Gunnerside Gill, or from Surrender Bridge, or near Langthwaite and Booze. The National Park also organises conducted walks for those interested in lead mining, with an expert who will be able to answer all their questions about the industry. Before looking at old workings it is well worth while visiting the Folk Museum in Reeth where the methods of mining are illustrated by clear diagrams and a display of the tools used and also by the end product, an ingot of lead. It must be emphasized that no attempt to explore old workings should ever be made as they are now extremely unstable and dangerous, and any area with old shafts should be approached with caution as these were covered in the past with old timbers which may well be rotten by now.

Building for God's Work

Foursquare and solid, chapels and former chapels are to be found in all the villages. There are Anglican churches too, most restored in Victorian days, but it has been estimated that, in the C19th, while 60% of people in Richmond attended the Anglican church, perhaps only 10% of people in Swaledale did so.

The first non-conformists in Swaledale date back to the days of the Puritans. The owner of the manor of Healaugh was Philip, Lord Wharton, who became a strong advocate of the Puritan cause and a friend of Oliver Cromwell (See section, 'Famous People in the Dale'). Wharton built a small chapel at Smarber near Low Row and although this no longer exists a tablet has been put up on the site to commemorate the first independent chapel in Swaledale. Wharton used his land at Healaugh to found a charity to provide bibles for poor non-conformist children in his various estates.

There is a Quaker Lane in Richmond and a Quaker Close in Reeth and the large school building with its decorative roof to the west of Reeth was built with Quaker money in the last century. This sect, too, dates from Puritan days, when George Fox, believing that God speaks direct to the individual, rejected 'steeple houses', as he called churches. The name 'Quaker' was first applied to Fox in derision when he bade people tremble at the word of the Lord. They called themselves 'Friends of the Truth'. or later just 'Friends'. At first, suspected of promoting sedition, Quakers were fined or imprisoned for refusing to attend church. On one occasion at Healaugh the Quakers' possessions were seized and given to the poor, who immediately returned them to their former owners. When the law permitted, they built modest meeting houses. One Quaker family left money to build the school at Reeth, not without opposition from the local Anglican and Methodist schools. The Friends' school accepted children from any sect and the older children could learn surveying, mining and geology, as well as more conventional subjects.

The Anglican churches had little appeal for the mining community. The custom of allowing people to buy pews, as in Muker where every pew was private, discouraged newcomers and poorer families. Rectors frequently lived elsewhere, leaving the care of the parish to a poorly paid curate. Churches were visibly neglected. Holy Trinity church in Richmond was derelict, St. Mary's Parish church was described as filthy and the church in Arkengarthdale reported to be ruinous in 1814.

In 1761 John Wesley himself came to Swaledale but by then Jacob Rowell and his friends at Newbiggin in Teesdale had already spread Wesley's message. These men came from the same background as the miners. They told, in words the miners could understand, how they themselves had been converted, and they preached that in the sight of God it was not worldly position that mattered but simple faith and an honest and sober life. "The Society is one of the most lively I have met with in England", Wesley wrote of one visit, and of another, "I preached in Swaledale to a loving people, increasing both in grace and number".

The money to build the Methodist chapels came out of the pockets of the miners, and their hands often helped to carry the stones of which they were built. Not everyone, of course, was a Methodist but records speak of miners "pouring down the craggy hills" to services and the finest chapels stand in villages where lead mining flourished. Built with the doorway in the gable end, they are sober buildings, for unnecessary elaboration would not have been approved, but proud testimonies to the faith and devotion of their people. That at Langthwaite with its classical pillared doorway and round arched windows offers an interesting contrast with the decorative and traditional Anglican church nearby. The dignified chapel at Gunnerside, in a very similar style, was built to hold a congregation of 500. "Earnest, loving and simple people", Wesley described them, and their enthusiasm was kept up with dramatic preaching and fervent hymn singing while their community built its life round regular class meetings, Mothers' groups, choirs, Sunday School for children, chapel teas and special anniversaries. The mine owners, not surprisingly, looked with favour on this religion which preached the virtue of hard work and, in particular, sobriety.

The Literary Institute at Muker, with its most attractive gable end, and other institutes at Keld, Gunnerside, Reeth and elsewhere, show the general enthusiasm for adult education which was a feature of Victorian days. These institutes provided libraries for quiet reading as well as evenings of lectures, discussions and music, and were well supported by the local community.

The fall in population left many of these chapels and other buildings without followers and some have found new uses, some as dwelling houses, though their former status can still be recognised.

18th Century Elegance

The stockings knitted in the Dales went through the market at Richmond and included 2000 dozen pairs a year for export, chiefly to Holland. In 1826 'Paterson's Roads', a directory of English towns, stated, "Richmond has one of the greatest corn markets in the county. Being seated on the utmost verge of the district in which grain is produced, the cornfactors and millers repair hither from Swaledale and Wensleydale and other parts of the moors." Butchers were given special facilities in Richmond where cattle from Scotland and the Dales were sold at fortnightly markets. An ancillary trade was in leather goods, shoes, gloves, saddles and bridles. The Green was originally a small industrial centre with a tannery, a corn-mill, a brewery, a fulling mill and dye works, all needing water from the river. Teams of pack-horses brought lead from the mining areas to Richmond to be sent on to manufacturing towns like Stockton and Hull and dealing in lead added to the wealth of Richmond's merchants.

The story of the gradual development of Richmond is well set out on the top floor of the Richmondshire Museum. In 1756 an imposing town hall was built and 25 years later the market-place itself, the largest horse-shoe market in England, was re-cobbled and the old market cross replaced by a tall obelisk. The medieval houses which surrounded the market place were swept away and the present houses built. The intrusion of modern shop-fronts has altered their appearance at street level but the upper floors still retain their Georgian elegance with tall windows and symmetrical design. Stone is the natural building material of the area but some of these buildings are in brick, chosen to enhance their design, as in the sumptuous King's Head Hotel with its contrasting stonework and classical doorways. The architect John Carr, who built Harewood House, was surveyor of bridges to the North Riding and it was he who built the beautiful arched Richmond Bridge in 1789.

The well-to-do people of Richmond also built fine houses for their families, as a walk to the cobbled end of Frenchgate will show. There was not space enough in the town centre and some of the grandest houses were built in Newbiggin. In this spacious and tree-lined, and still cobbled, street there is an interesting variety of Georgian building styles, from a house with classical pillared portico and pediments over its windows to one in a picturesque 'Gothic' style with bay windows and pointed arches. Rising above the trees is Culloden Tower, an 18th century 'folly', with stone fretwork and pinnacles, built to commemorate the victory over the Jacobites led by Bonnie Prince Charlie.

Richmond with its flourishing market but only a few small industries was becoming a centre for people who disliked the growing industrial towns. "The atmosphere is never polluted with the smoke of steam engines and other noxious vapours", wrote Christopher Clarkson in 1821, and "The demand for houses of a genteel description is now very great".

Good society likes to have sophisticated entertainment and it was in 1788 that a theatre was built. Situated just off the market place, the theatre remains a perfect small Georgian playhouse, the most complete example in the country, with green-painted boxes, gallery, pit and remarkably deep stage. It is possible to make a tour of the dressing rooms, stage and auditorium.

Horse racing was another pastime enjoyed by the people of Richmond. North Yorkshire had long been famous for its horses, "All this country is full of jockeys, that is to say, dealers in horses and breeders of horses," wrote Defoe in 1727. "I do believe that some of the gallopers of this county will outdo for speed and strength the swiftest horse that ever was bred in Turkey or Barbary". Racing became immensely popular with the local gentry who often entered their own horses. The old race-course and the Georgian starter's box can still be seen. To coincide with the races grand assemblies were held in the new Town Hall and in the King's Head Hotel.

Clarkson summed up Richmond very happily, "The Society is good, chiefly composed of persons of independent fortunes who at a moderate rate enjoy all the advantages of a polished and agreeable intercourse".

Reeth, too, was flourishing, as its large cobbled market space shows. Roads were improved and the bridge rebuilt by Carr. Here, too, houses were built in the new elegant style, one of fine stone with a classical doorway, others with plastered and painted fronts which still add brightness to the town today, with three storeys and tall symmetrical windows. A variety of classical and decorative doorways are to be seen in a walk around Reeth. Flourishing trade warranted the building of a new hotel, grander than the old inns. Draycott Hall, visible through a gateway at Fremington, and Marske Hall are other examples of fine houses built at this time.

Stone Houses and Stone Walls

The oldest existing houses in Swaledale, sometimes with the date carved in stone, were built in the 17th century, their windows having stone mullions and sometimes dripstones, and were originally one room deep, for a double depth house did not become common until the C19th. Some of the most attractive are the farmhouses and farm buildings under one long roof. In upper Swaledale almost every meadow has its own small barn (See section,'The Farmer's Life') and these are among the most notable features of the landscape.

People's needs change over the years and they alter, divide or enlarge their houses. Some have obviously been extended, with a slightly different roof or windows, possibly for another member of the family. When lead mining brought more and more people, numerous very small dwellings were built. Some were cottages in small groups on the fell, of which only a few stones remain, and others are the mixed rows and terraces of very small houses found in Arkengarthdale and elsewhere and which crowd the space in Gunnerside. Too small for today's living standards, two or more may now be combined. Outbuilding at the back, new doors and porches are often added to older houses. Reeth, once a flourishing market town, has some noticeably grander houses.

All the houses were built of local sandstone, usually quarried nearby, and roofed with the thinner flagstones from the Yoredale series, called grey slates. These can be as much as a metre long, the size diminishing as the roof rises, and each one is held in place by just one wooden peg. An excellent explanation of the building tradition is displayed in the Folk Museum at Reeth, along with one of the huge roofing slabs.

A view from a hillside down on to the Dale reveals a fascinating network of stone walls. The pattern of farming in the Middle Ages was to work large communal fields in strips and any enclosing of land usually led to disputes. But by the C16th villagers had begun to enclose small plots near their homes. The walls of these little fields make a crazed pattern near villages, winding over irregular ground and turning to meet another wall, and were often built of stones cleared from the field itself. Gunnerside is remarkable for the preservation of the early field walls and a walk along the footpaths to the north of the village will reveal how small the fields are and how irregular the walls, contrasting with the straight lines of the walls on the opposite hillside.

By the C17th, farming in communal fields had died out and people were exchanging strips and buying others, to make independent farms. In this way the old communal fields were divided and farmers built walls round their own holdings. These fields are found on good land on the lower slopes and level ground and are larger than the earliest plots but are still of irregular shape with walls that curve or take a sudden bend to meet another wall. Small additional intakes on the moorland edge were often made by miners.

By the C18th, although the best land had already been divided and walled, there were still the unfenced commons on high ground. This was the era of improvements in farming practice, with new methods of drilling and sowing, draining, manuring, liming, breeding of improved stock and growing turnips for winter feed, with the result that the weights of sheep and cattle sold at Smithfield had doubled by the end of the century. Enclosure of land for scientific management became the fashion, led by men like Sir Thomas Elliott of Fremington, described by the great advocate of the new ideas, Arthur Young, as one of the greatest improvers of moors in Yorkshire. He advised "never to attempt any improvement without enclosing".

Permission to enclose commons required an Act of Parliament, but this was easily obtained by a few well-to-do landowners. These enclosures were mapped out on paper first, often with scant regard for the terrain, and created the long arrow-straight walls up the hillsides. The road from Marske to Reeth goes through an area of these geometrically regular fields. The growing population could not have been fed without more productive farming methods, but these enclosures deprived people of the commons grazing, as Young himself realised, "The poor man can only say, I had a cow and Parliament has taken it from me". Many of these walls were built by full-time wallers.

To make a good wall, sods are removed and the bottom course laid on firm subsoil. On either side the larger stones face outwards while the middle is filled with smaller stones. Lines of longer through-stones key the wall together. About a metre wide at the base, it narrows gradually to the top, where a line of coping stones is set on edge. To build a dry-stone wall on sloping ground is a work of art, which allows the wall to give and settle with the ground. Visitors are asked never to climb over walls, for even one stone dislodged will eventually destroy the balance of all the others.

Market Day in the country town of Richmond from the Castle Keep

Richmond lies close to, but not on, the main lines of communication. The Stockton and Darlington railway was opened in 1825, and the main line subsequently ran through York to London. But a branch line to Richmond was not built until 1846. Projected lines further up the dale to Reeth were never built, and the line to Richmond itself was closed, like so many others, in 1969. The old station has now been converted into a farm and garden centre. Even in the C18th Richmond found itself aside from major thoroughfares, for the Great North Road, now the A1, lay at some distance, and the new turnpike road (a road paid for by the tolls of users) across the Pennines to Brough took its way through Stainmore well to the north, a route followed centuries before by the Romans, and today the main A66 road from Scotch Corner.

Richmond, in consequence, has remained one of the smaller English towns. It still has no noxious manufactures and it is still a place of agreeable intercourse, as its historian Christopher Clarkson reported in 1821. A view from the castle will show that there has been a considerable amount of new house building around the outskirts, but even the Normans would still be able to see their old market place with its radiating streets, and ghosts from the C18th would have no difficulty in recognising their old homes.

The town has remained a local market and service centre for the area and it also now has close associations with the army. Since 1873 Richmond has been the home town of the famous Yorkshire regiment, the Green Howards, who fought for King William at the battle of the Boyne and have since distinguished themselves in many engagements through the years, to the Falklands War. At one time regiments were known by the name of their commanding officer. There were two regiments commanded by two Colonels Howard, and to distinguish one from the other, that led by Charles Howard wore green facings on their uniforms and became known as the Green Howards while the others were the Buff Howards. Their beautiful museum is in the old Trinity church. MOD warning signs are seen in parts of Swaledale. In the early years of this century Lord Baden Powell had his headquarters in Richmond and he suggested Catterick as a suitable site for military training.

Richmond now provides hotels, guest houses and other facilities for the increasing number of tourists who find the town a good centre for exploring this part of North Yorkshire.

Tourists, too, are playing an increasing part in the economics of Swaledale. Here the closure of the lead mines in the early years of this century led to a dramatic and rapid fall in population, and the gradual mechanisation of farm work has reduced the number of men needed for agriculture, the other main source of livelihood in both Swaledale and Arkengarthdale. It has become increasingly difficult for young people to find employment in their local area. There is no large industry in either of the Dales today, nor is there any of the quarrying found in other parts of the Pennines. There are some craft enterprises, mainly directed toward the tourist, and service to tourists, in shops, pubs and places to stay, now adds to the income of many in the Dales. The people whose families have lived here for generations are proud of their dale and always welcome visitors who appreciate it, but they would be reluctant to see its economy entirely dependent on this source.

Farming remains the main use of the land, as modern farm buildings on the lower ground and the large numbers of sheep on the moorland testify, but it is increasingly difficult to get a good economic return from this without resorting to modern practices which alter the character of the landscape.

Fewer people meant that many houses were left empty and deteriorating until the recent growth of tourism. Many are now second homes for people whose employment is elsewhere or holiday cottages only in use for part of the year. People who visit Reeth on a busy weekend in the tourist season would find it difficult to imagine how quiet it can be in winter. In summer, serious walkers with boots and knapsacks are to be seen daily on the Pennine Way or the Coast to Coast Walk, and a host of other holiday makers enjoy a stroll through the flowering meadows, gaze with interest at the old lead-mining remains, sit on the green at Reeth, explore the craft shops in the villages, and visit in real life places previously familiar from the TV screen.

The increased number of people who enjoy walking and climbing has led to the formation of the Swaledale Mountain Rescue Organisation, with its headquarters at Marske. All the people who form this are volunteers from the local area, and the funds needed to maintain the service are collected from voluntary donations. Visitors who see a collecting box may like to remember that the unexpected accident can happen to even the most careful.

The picturesque setting of the 12th Century Marrick Priory in Swaledale

The Swale Below Richmond

The River Swale continues on its way beyond Richmond to Catterick Bridge. So far it has run through a steep-sided valley, descending some 305 metres (1000 ft) in a course of about 30 miles. Below Catterick Bridge the character of the river changes, for now it flows quietly, with many meanders, through the level and fertile soil of the plain of York until it unites with the River Ure to form the Ouse.

The village of **BROMPTON ON SWALE** is on a bend of the river, popular with anglers, some three miles from Richmond. It is recorded in the Domesday Book as Brunton, and the medieval hospital of St. Giles was nearby. Today it is a pleasant mixture of old and new building, with a well appointed caravan park, and makes a good centre for a holiday, being within easy reach of both Swaledale and Wensleydale.

CATTERICK was once a Roman town, for the Romans built a fort, Cataractonium, around which a flourishing civilian settlement developed. Catterick, too, was famous in the early days of Christianity, for here Paulinus is said to have baptised more than ten thousand people in 625 AD. Today it is a pleasant place with two greens, the lower one being spacious with one side bordered by trees and a stream. To the north of the village is the famous Catterick Bridge racecourse.

The site of the army garrison nearby was originally recommended by Lord Baden Powell in 1908 when he was asked to suggest suitable ground for a military training area, but it was not until 1924 that the Royal Corps of Signals arrived, an advance party of 'Catterick Camp' as it became known to thousands of soldiers and their families. Today it presents many aspects of a town rather than of a garrison. There are necessarily many barracks and parade grounds, but since the 1960s there has been increased emphasis on good housing for families and on recreation facilities. Sports of all kinds, including an indoor ski slope, are available, and in many places recreation fields, mature trees and carefully mown grass give the impression of a well-maintained suburban area rather than of a military establishment. Large tracts of land have been reserved for military exercises, firing ranges and tank training, and visitors will see the M.O.D. signs.

In the churchyard at **BOLTON ON SWALE** is the tombstone of Henry Jenkins, 'the modern Methuselah', who claimed to have been born in 1501 at nearby Ellerton upon Swale and who died at Bolton in 1670, aged 169! He is said to have swum across the Swale when he was 100. Once as a witness at York Assizes he was able to confirm that certain tithes had, to his personal knowledge, been paid for 120 years. The story goes that a lawyer in search of evidence in a legal case sought advice. On arriving at the cottage where Jenkins lived he saw an old white-haired man sitting in the garden. On being questioned, the man replied, 'You'd better ask my father'. The visitor entered the cottage where he found an old, old man bent over the fire. 'You'd better ask my father,' said this old man too, 'He's chopping sticks out the back.' And there indeed was Henry Jenkins aged 166.

The nearby village of **SCORTON** has a walled village green, a most unusual and possibly unique feature. The grammar school was founded in the C18th and there is a Hospital of St. John of God which still carries on its traditional work. The name of Scorton is well known to many people who have never visited Yorkshire for it is the original home of the famous Scorton Arrow, one of the most prestigious archery contests in the world and generally acknowledged to be the oldest. This contest for the longbow certainly dates back to 1693 when it was first recorded but there can be little doubt that it was in existence long before this date.

A short distance from **ELLERTON UPON SWALE** are the grounds of **KIPLIN HALL**, a great sweep of parkland with trees, water and woodland. There are two nature trails and plenty of space to picnic. A Charitable Trust was established in 1968 to preserve and restore this most unusual C17th house, built of red brick and stone with two projecting towers crowned by octagonal domes. It was built by George Calvert, Lord Baltimore, who was the founder of the State of Maryland in the U.S.A., and the Historical Society of Maryland in America is among the contributors to the funds for restoration. In summer the house is open to visitors on some days in the week.

To the north of Richmond on a tributary of the Swale is the village of **GILLING WEST**, most attractive with stone houses and gardens. This village was an important place before Richmond Castle was built. It was a seat of government in the time of the Anglo-Saxons and is noted in the Domesday Book as having a parish church. Alan Rufus, the Norman, however, rejected it as a site for his castle and chose instead the more defensible position on the rock where Richmond now stands. Nearby is the private property of Aske Hall, the scene of a painting by the artist Turner.

The Farmer's Life

The distinctive landscape of Swaledale has been made by farming. It is only regular mowing which produces meadows full of flowers and cropping by animals which keeps pastures smooth and green, for unused land soon reverts to coarse grass and scrub. In the past, farmers expected to be largely self-sufficient and meadow, pasture and moorland were all used to the best advantage.

In early times the people grew all their crops but as transport improved this became unnecessary and Swaledale concentrated on pastoral farming. The fertile low ground grew tall grass to be mown for hay, an absolute essential for winter feeding, and on the slopes well-drained soil with a high lime content produced good grass for animals to crop. Even the moorland could provide food for hardy sheep and, in the days when most needs were met locally, peat to be cut, dried and carried home for the fire.

The old farmsteads are scattered about the Dale, always near water, with a house and a cluster of farm buildings. The farmer and his family, which might include unmarried relatives, usually did all the work. Most farms in the Dale kept both cattle and sheep, though farmers whose land lay largely on the lower slopes would be able to keep more cattle, while those in the upper reaches of the Dale depended more on their flocks of sheep.

Most sheep seen today on the moorland are Swaledale, with black faces and grey noses. These, as the name implies, were bred in this area and are remarkable for their ability to survive the winter and to live off the poor ground with little extra feeding. The moorland is open but a flock is 'heafed', trained in the past to keep to its own part of the fell, and this habit is passed through the lambs of the following generations. If a farm is sold, its 'heafed' sheep may well be sold with it.

The number of sheep on the common ground is regulated by a local committee, each farmer having so many 'gaits', the right to graze one sheep and its lambs. Although moorland looks wild, it needs to be carefully managed for over-grazing or under-grazing will alter the vegetation. Swaledale sheep can always find something to eat out on the fell unless there is very heavy snow, though in winter they are given some hay in addition and can be seen coming in a long line toward the feeding point at the appropriate time. At lambing time in April they are brought down closer to the farmhouse, so that the farmer may have them under his eye, and nowadays many are kept under cover for lambing. Sheep and lambs then go back on to the fell and at this time of year drivers need to be especially careful on unfenced roads, for a lamb has no experience of vehicles and, when alarmed, always runs to its mother, regardless of the fact that this may be straight in front of a car.

Visitors always enjoy watching a farmer gather up his flock with the help of one or two dogs. The ability to gather sheep is inherited and a good dog is prized because any puppies may be equally clever. These small black and white collies came originally from the Borders, possibly with drovers. They control the sheep with their eyes as much as by their movements and can divide the flock or even separate out a single sheep if required. Demonstrations of sheep-dogs' work at local events are always very popular. Local dogs are never seen wandering on their own, and farmers always ask visitors to keep all dogs under control for a ewe frightened by a dog may lose a lamb later even if she appears unharmed at the time.

Sheep are gathered off the moor when the old wool 'rises' as new wool grows, because this indicates the time for shearing. The shearer clips close to the skin so that the whole fleece stays in one piece and can be rolled up and tied, although the 'doddings', dirty pieces near the tail, are kept separate. The sheep look very naked for a few days but new wool grows remarkably quickly. Sheep have to be gathered in again for dipping which is compulsory, with dates fixed by the Ministry of Agriculture, to control sheep scab.

The wool of the Swaledale sheep, which has to shrug off winter weather, is coarse and used mainly for carpets. Most male lambs, wethers, are sold on to be fattened for butchers, but young females, gimmers, being hardy and also good mothers, are used for cross-breeding, often with blue-faced Leicesters, sheep with high arched noses and long ears, sometimes to be seen on the lower ground in the Dale. Their 'mule' offspring produce good lambs for the meat trade. A great sheep fair is held each May at Tan Hill, and is well worth a visit, for the finest Swaledale sheep will be there.

The farmer in the past used the high ground and the moorland for sheep. On the lower pasture he kept cows and it was the need to accommodate cows that led to the building of the numerous small barns which are so characteristic a part of the Swaledale landscape, and which are found only in the Yorkshire Dales.

In early days all children inherited equally and land was often divided, while miners, too, were often small-holders, so that a farmer might have only a little more than a hectare of good land. Caring for and milking cows is time-consuming work but suited a man with a family who could help, and the sale of butter and cheese would mean a quick return and a steady income.

Cows cannot live outside in winter, and each small barn was built to accommodate four, while the hay essential for their winter feed could be stored in the loft. The slits in the walls were made to ensure ventilation, for hay can heat up in a confined space and even take light spontaneously. In late spring the cows would be put out on the higher pastures and the manure made during the winter spread on the meadows to ensure a good crop of grass for hay. And with the grass came the flowers, so brilliant a part of Swaledale's summer.

Milking was done by hand, in the barn in winter, though at times cows would be dry before the next calf was born, or out in the fields in summer. It could take a month to teach a young cow to stand still in an open field. Back-cans, with one side flat and specially made to carry home the milk, are to be seen in the local museum. The best cheese was made from the rich milk from cows on summer pastures while the milk later in the year was mainly used for butter. The cheese and the butter were sold at market or collected by regular agents and even supplied the London markets.

Late summer was hay-time, a vital operation because the amount of hay absolutely determined how many cows could be kept through winter, and they would be the main source of income for the future. When mowing had to be done with scythes, extra men might be hired and all the family would help to spread the hay to dry in the sun. Being able to store it in a field barn saved a great deal of carrying. After mowing, the grass grows quickly for a while and the cows would be put to graze this 'fog' before going back into the barns again for winter.

Each cow would have had a calf early in the year and these would have been well fed, sometimes on the skim milk from butter-making until the autumn cattle sales. The farmer's year followed a traditional pattern, with calving, lambing, peat-cutting, shearing, dipping, hay-making, and each day had a succession of milking, cheese-making and butter-churning.

Our life-time has seen a revolution in farming methods comparable to that in the 18th century. Cows today are milked by machine in large milking parlours and the milk collected in tankers by the Milk Marketing Board. Calves are reared intensively in huge sheds, often indoors all year round. Modern barns are a distinctive feature of Swaledale today, particularly noticeable where there is little other new building. Hay is mown and baled by machines and transported readily wherever it is required. There is no need to keep it in a building in the meadow itself. Indeed, hay itself is not essential. The need for winter feed still exists but this is more easily obtained by fertilizing and cutting green grass for silage. The grass does not have to be dried so there is no worry about the weather and a field will often produce more feed this way than if left to grow hay. But a field heavily fertilized with nitrogen to produce a crop of lush green grass grows no flowers. Machines work quickly and save labour, but stone walls round small fields can be very inconvenient and steep slopes, where a man might have scythed in the past, may be dangerous for a tractor. Difficult land becomes abandoned and rushes and scrub creep in.

All visitors who come to the Dales admire the green pastures and flower-filled meadows, the stone walls and small barns, but the question arises whether the farmer can be expected to accept a reduced yield from his land so that flowers can be left to grow, or to pay for the repair of a stone barn which is no longer of use to him.

The value of this traditional landscape is seen in its inclusion in the Yorkshire Dales National Park. Government grants are given to hill farmers to assist them to continue farming on difficult land and the upper end of Swaledale has been designated an Environmentally Sensitive Area where special grants can be available for people who agree to use only specified amounts of fertilizer and not to cut the grass for hay or silage until a fixed date after the flowers have seeded. The Yorkshire Dales National Park is exploring the possibility of alternative uses for some of the redundant but attractive barns and it is hoped that assistance with their repair and with the maintenance of stone walls may be forthcoming. Even so, returns on hard work are meagre and it is thanks to the efforts of the National Park and to the co-operation of local farmers, who value their Dale, that this unique landscape can be preserved for us all to enjoy.

By Moorland, Meadows and Woods

Wide and windswept moorland, flower-filled meadows and sheltered woods, they are all to be found in Swaledale and the best way to enjoy them is on foot, if possible. It is only the walker who can, in fact, see the spectacular Kisdon Gorge and some of the finest waterfalls, or appreciate the rough heather, the velvety grass of an old track, or the tall flowers brushing alongside a stone-flagged trod through the hay-fields.

The Pennine Way comes down from Great Shunner Fell to Thwaite, round the flank of Kisdon Hill to Keld and then up to Tan Hill. This magnificent trail, Kisdon Hill being one of its most enjoyable stretches, crosses only the top end of Swaledale. To get an impression of the whole dale it would be better to follow Wainwright's Coast to Coast Walk, for this enters Swaledale at the head and, keeping to the northern slopes, follows down the Dale, taking in moorland, old lead-mining areas and farmland, to Reeth and on to Richmond, the only town he visits.

Whether walking or driving on one of the moorland roads, visitors can enjoy superb panoramic views and look down on the winding river and the patchwork of fields. The moorland is on millstone grit, a durable rock on which waterlogged vegetation has decayed to form a blanket of peat, where heather mixed with bilberry flourishes, where the white bobbles of cotton grass flower in wetter places and where sphagnum moss grows on really boggy ground. The wide open spaces change colour with the seasons, the heather, much loved by insects on a warm day, flowering purple in late summer, and the bracken, undesirable plant though it may be, bright green in spring and rusty brown in autumn sunlight.

To enjoy the exhilarating moorland, it is not necessary to be a long distance walker, for a round walk of five miles or so from Reeth could include Reeth Low Moor, or a similar distance from Muker or Keld take in the grassy track of the old Corpse Way and the spectacular river gorge, where trees crowd close to the water's edge. One warning, though: however promising the day seems to be, make sure to take some warm and windproof clothing, for weather can change quickly and there is often a breeze on high ground, which may spoil an otherwise lovely walk. Long-distance walks on open moorland should never be undertaken without careful preparation, proper footwear and clothing, and someone with a knowledge of map and compass reading, for mist can come down unexpectedly.

Swaledale sheep grazing on the roadside in Arkengarthdale

The picturesque village of Reeth sited in beautiful Swaledale

There are many places on the moors where drivers can pull in and stop at the side of the road. They are asked to remember, however, that although the ground is not fenced the public do not have any right to go on to, or to wander over, moorland. Walkers should keep to the sign-posted paths or rights of way and dogs must be kept under close control. Even the best behaved dog can suddenly take it into its head to chase after sheep, while the grass tussocks and heather are nesting places for many birds, lapwings, curlews, redshanks and others which come to the moors to breed, as well as the grouse which are part of the Dales' economy. Fires must never be lit and it is important never to drop matches or cigarette ends for heather can catch fire easily and even the underlying peat will smoulder, causing disastrous damage over a wide area.

The visitor comes down from the moorland through grassy pastures bounded by stone walls, the heather is left behind and bushes of hawthorn, and sometimes blackthorn, grow by the wayside and birch and rowan trees cling to steep slopes. Most people stop for a while to admire the many waterfalls of the upper dale. Wainwath Force, where the water flows over wide steps, is near the road, and Kisdon Force, in a deep gorge can be reached

by a short walk from Keld. These are two famous falls but visitors will find many others in the steep-sided valleys or gills, where the water hurries down the slopes, for instance pretty cascades near Thwaite or a fine fall behind the old smelt mill in Swinnergill.

Some of the minor roads on the slopes of both Swaledale and Arkengarthdale, originally made with only a few local farmers' vehicles in mind, are very narrow, and drivers who are apprehensive about the paintwork on their cars may prefer to avoid them for there is little space to pass an oncoming vehicle. The main routes present few problems though at peak holiday times drivers may need to be patient and parking in some of the more popular villages may be scarce. Reeth has plenty of space and a lovely green.

The name Swale means 'rushing, swirling river' and its moods vary from silvery water on a sunny day sliding over gravel beds or splashing down stepped waterfalls, to a brown torrent surging past and breaking into creamy foam. The steep sides of the Dale allow water to run off very fast and heavy rain up in the hills can cause the river to rise suddenly, even as far down as Richmond. Advance flood warning notices should never be ignored.

For those with no desire to do more than go for a gentle stroll, the lower ground offers endless pleasures. In early summer the meadows are golden with buttercups while the hedges and verges are white with flowering hawthorn, cow parsley and sweet cicely. On a sunny day the air is redolent with the scent of the hawthorn blossoms or the wild garlic in the woods, while the crushed leaves of sweet cicely give off a sharp aniseed flavour. The larger, brighter flowers on the verges and grasslands catch the eye, especially the bright pink campion or, later, the blue cranesbill, but the observant visitor will also find tiny yellow and purple pansies, white daisies, blue speedwell, yellow trefoils and many others.

The hay meadows are of such great botanical interest that the Yorkshire Wildlife Trust now has a nature reserve at Yellands Meadow near Muker. In most parts of England today fields are ploughed and grass sown to be heavily fertilized and cut for silage, so that they become a uniform green with no flowers. Because meadows in the Dale are left to grow hay and have received little artificial fertilizer they still produce an abundance of flowers, not only the yellow buttercups but white pignut, blue cranesbill, pink clover and numerous other varieties. A really lovely walk from Gunnerside goes through flowering meadows by a series of stiles to Muker, and there are similar paths near Thwaite and Angram. It must be remembered that hay is a vital crop for local farmers and they ask walkers to keep in single file through it. Arkengarthdale is equally beautiful with a network of paths alongside flowering meadows and over streams.

The Dales have a number of plants of particular interest to the flower enthusiast, including varieties of orchid, the globe flower (trollius), and the melancholy thistle, which does not occur in the south of England. The National Park organises a number of special interest walks, led by an expert, for lovers of flowers.

The flowers are seen at their best in early summer but even after they have faded the long seed heads of the grasses wave and ripple in the wind, a variety of feathery bents, spindly fescues, soft cats-tails and Yorkshire fog, so quickly bowed down by dew or mist. Whatever the time of year, there is always something to be found and appreciated.

Walkers will find inexpensive maps with the footpaths clearly marked available in many shops and also leaflets of suggested walks produced by the National Park Authority with interesting notes on the way. They are invited, also, to join a guided walk with one of the National Park wardens.

The meadow flowers are at their most spectacular in early summer; late summer displays the wide expanses of purple heather and autumn is no less colourful. Birch and rowan trees grow on the thin soils of the high ground, colouring yellow and red against the white limestone scars. The lower part of the Dale is as beautiful as the upper. Here the main road winds through a series of hills where patches of green fields on the less steep slopes alternate with woods crowned by high limestone edges. On the more fertile ground the trees are larger, with heavy-leaved sycamore and the more elegant ash being common. Many woods are mixed, with some dark evergreen trees adding to the colours of spring and autumn. The natural vegetation includes bushes of juniper, along with Scots pine and yew the only conifers native to Britain. Footpaths near woodland include Thirnswood Gill, a deliberately planted piece of woodland in Swaledale, and woods near Langthwaite, and the steps used in former days to reach Marrick village from the Priory go through a wood full of wild flowers in spring.

A footpath from Richmond Bridge leads to the beautiful National Trust property of Billy Banks Wood above the river, and there is a very pleasant walk through woods and fields from Richmond to the ruins of Easby Abbey. It is also possible to walk and picnic in Whitcliffe Wood to the west of Richmond. There are magnificent views of Richmond, perhaps at their best in autumn when the castle keep rises above the browns, yellows and reds of the trees in the wooded gorge. From the viewpoint on Beacon Hill it is possible to look across the great plain to the towers of York Minster.

Older children much enjoy a visit to the Falls on the river below Richmond castle, where the water runs over a series of stepped rocks and pools, where hardy people can splash about. Ronaldshay park is a pleasant town park with a children's play area, and Friary Gardens are beautiful with formal bedding. St. Nicholas, first planted in 1910, with interesting species rhododendrons and a border of shrub roses is a garden for connoisseurs.

One last warning: midges by the million hatch out in summer, particularly near water or in sheltered places under trees, and anyone who wants to enjoy a warm summer evening is advised to take plenty of insect repellent.

In the early days when large tracts of land in Swaledale and Arkengarthdale were reserved as hunting forest by the Normans, the woods would have been full of all kinds of animals, deer, boars, wolves, hares, foxes, badgers and otters. The growth of population through the centuries and the gradual change from a wild to a farming environment drove many away. The last wolf in England was killed in the 16th century. There are records of red deer in Swaledale as late as the 17th century but the great industry that sprang up around the lead mines, and the cutting down of trees for fuel further restricted the habitat for wild creatures. Today there are a few roe deer in some of the woods but these are seldom seen, and the visitor is not very likely to see even the small mammals, fieldmice, hedgehogs and voles, which still live in the fields. The more commonly seen rabbit would not have been here in the early days of the Norman forests for it was not introduced into England until the 12th century for the sake of its meat.

The woods, particularly in the lower end of Swaledale, are full of birds, too many to list here, their songs heard more often than they themselves are seen. Birds of open field and moorland are more easily seen and are of great interest to the visitor from lowland country. The commonest of these is seldom noticed, for it spends much of its time on the ground. The meadow pipit is a small brown bird with a creamy streaked breast and it makes its nest in the tussocky grass.

The pied wagtail is common but visitors may also see a yellow wagtail. Not to be confused with the grey wagtail which has a yellow breast but a grey back, this less common bird is bright yellow with a brownish green back, and, unlike the others, is a migrant, spending the winter in West Africa and coming to Britain to breed, arriving in late April or early May. The wheatear is another visitor from Africa. Of the same family as the robin its prominent white rump is very noticeable as it darts away quickly, dipping low over the ground, when startled. In the past, thousands of migrating wheatears used to be trapped as they crossed the South Coast, for they were a special delicacy on smart dinner tables.

The lapwings, or pee-wits, those most elegant and decorative birds with the curled crest, spend the winter on marshes and mud-flats close to the sea, and their arrival in Swaledale means that winter is coming to an end. They make their nests among the grassy tussocks, amongst which their chicks can later be seen running like mice while the agitated parents scream and flutter at a distance, to draw attention away from their offspring. Their 'plovers' eggs' used to be considered a special treat and every year hundreds were collected to be sent to London, until an act for the protection of lapwings was passed in 1928 which put an end to this trade.

The alarm call of the curlew is so distinctive that it is easily recognised by most people. These birds, the largest of the waders, with long legs and long curving bill, also spend the winter on low ground but come to the moorland to breed, making a nest in a hollow lined with grass or heather. The redshank, the greenshank and the oyster-catcher, also come to nest on the moors.

But the real birds of the moorland are the red grouse, for they remain all the year round, their main food being the heather, above which their heads can often be seen. Red grouse are found only in Britain and to preserve them for sportsmen the moors are carefully looked after by keepers. Predators are kept down and controlled burning of patches of heather is done in March, to ensure new growth for the young birds in the following year. The nest is just a scrape in the ground lined with grass or heather. Walkers seldom get close to grouse but birds of all kinds often remain remarkably unalarmed by a car, and if a grouse is close to the edge of the road it is possible to see that its legs and feet are covered with feathers which help it to keep warm as it tramps down a space for itself in the snow in winter. A startled grouse flies low over the heather, the whirring of its wings making a distinctive sound.

Other carefully preserved birds are pheasants, which can sometimes be seen in Arkengarthdale. They were introduced into Britain from Asia, possibly by the Romans, and a number of different types have been added since the C18th. Pheasants are an easy prey for foxes and other predators, and careful game-keepers spend many hours looking after the woods as well as keeping away human poachers. Each year thousands of birds are raised in coops and released into the wild to keep up the numbers, and these birds are often little alarmed by people and not at all by cars.

Not all birds are summer visitors. Flocks of fieldfares and redwings fly in to the Dales from their breeding grounds in Northern Europe. When they land on a field and start to pick their way across it, winter is on the way.

Anyone who visits Richmond over the spring bank holiday weekend will find the town full of people enjoying themselves, for this is the traditional Richmond Meet Weekend. In 1892 the ardent cyclists of North Yorkshire and South Durham held the first meet, and a central part of the weekend is still a bicycle race round Richmond and over the bone-shaking cobbles of the market place. Cycling, however, now forms only a small part of a carnival weekend with football competitions, entertainments, displays, a procession, floats and music, in fact something for everyone, old and young, to enjoy. The Richmondshire Museum has an interesting display of photographs and mementoes of the old bicycling days.

This is Richmond's most spectacular occasion but there are others throughout the year, ranging from a St.George's Day parade to fireworks at the Castle in November. The First Fruits ceremony in the market place early in September dates back many centuries, and recalls the vital importance of the harvest to the people of past ages. A local farmer presents the mayor with a sample of corn from the year's harvest. This is examined by the millers and if it is satisfactory the farmer is given a bottle of wine. In addition to traditional ceremonies, English Heritage today sometimes recreate episodes from the past with convincing knights or Cavaliers.

Swaledale has two agricultural shows in summer, at Reeth and at Muker. These shows have a long tradition and are a highlight of the year for local people. Here the visitor can discover what a prize Swaledale sheep ought to look like, wonder at the size of onions and leeks on display, gaze enviously at the lines of perfectly baked cakes and scones, or admire the many fine knitting and craft displays. Special attractions and competitions add to the entertainment.

The Swaledale Festival, which lasts for a whole fortnight from late May, offers all kinds of entertainment. Events might include folk dancers from abroad, concerts of classical music by well-known artists, plays, choir singing, folk music, performances by Dales musicians and entertainments for all the family, as well as lectures, films and exhibitions. Among the performers will be Reeth Brass Band, reminding us that this music is traditional in the Dales and that each village once had its own band, though now only Muker and Reeth survive. Brass band concerts can still be enjoyed on some occasions in summer.

Richmond offers visitors performances by the local operatic, musical and dramatic societies. The Georgian Theatre invites visiting companies and artists, putting on a variety of plays and concerts, and a performance in this unique Georgian theatre is enhanced by the feeling that one is back in the C18th. It is possible at other times to visit the museum and do a tour of the dressing rooms, stage and auditorium.

People also have the opportunity to enjoy many outdoor and energetic sports. Richmond itself has a modern swimming pool, with separate teaching pool, in beautiful surroundings among trees, and a cafeteria and bar, where one can sit outside. The Sports Centre offers facilities for indoor games, badminton and table tennis, and a gymnasium. Though designed primarily for local clubs, facilities are available to the general public at weekends. There is an 18 hole golf course, a bowling green and a limited amount of fishing is possible in some places.

The Swaledale Outdoor Centre provides enthusiasts with the opportunity to compete in fell-walking, running, or canoeing for slalom or white-water championships. Other attractions include a Sports Day in Arkengarthdale and a marathon walk in Swaledale, and the rough ground of the lower dale provides suitable terrain for motor-cycle trials in autumn. For those who cannot see themselves running up a fell, the Yorkshire Dales National Park provides enjoyable and not too demanding guided walks.

No mention of sport in Swaledale would be complete without grouse shooting, and walkers on the moorland will come across the 'butts', where the 'guns' wait for the grouse to be driven toward them by a line of 'beaters'. Driven grouse fly extremely fast and it is said to be some of the most exciting and demanding shooting to be had. Only the very wealthy can afford a day's shooting but the sport is greatly in demand and is making an increasing contribution to the Dales' economy.

The Tourist Information Centre in Richmond publishes a list of day-to-day activities in Richmondshire and this is an invaluable guide to entertainments, shows and sporting events. The Yorkshire Dales National Park also provides a diary of events and a detailed list of their special interest guided walks. The visitor will find that there is something interesting going on each day.

Crafts Old and New

In the days when travel was difficult and money was scarce, the people of Swaledale expected to be self-sufficient in many ways. Local masons built houses of stone quarried nearby and doors and windows were all made by workmen in the Dale. Local joiners and wheelwrights supplied the carts, ploughs and hay-sweeps for the farm while the local blacksmith made the ploughshares, wheel-hoops and fire-grates. There was a fine tradition of cabinet making in the Dale and tables, chairs and cupboards used in the houses were made in Gunnerside and Richmond. The farmer himself would make his own creels of bent hazel rods, or besoms (brooms) from ling gathered on the moors. Some men could furnish the top of a stick with a ram's horn, softened by boiling, and carve it into a bird's head, a fish or animal. This skill is still practised today and such sticks are to be found in many shops. They are very popular with visitors, though not all seen today are made locally by hand.

Mats were made by the housewife, who cut old clothes into strips and then prodded or hooked them through a sacking base. They provided an excellent warm covering for a stone-flagged floor. Today newly made mats in this tradition can be found in some shops, though seldom as large as those made in the past. Quilts for the family's beds, also, were made at home, by stitching two layers of cloth together with a warm infilling. The layers of material were stretched over a large frame and then stitched all over, with one hand above and one below, in traditional patterns of chains, feathers, leaves and flowers against a background of diamonds. Old quilts still in good condition now fetch high prices as antiques. This is extremely skilful and time-consuming work and although there are still women able to make a quilt, it will be a costly item. In some places visitors may, however, find cushions quilted in the traditional patterns.

An earlier chapter in this guide has told of the history of knitting in Swaledale. Today at Swaledale Woollens in Muker the visitor will find a range of sweaters, cardigans and other knitted goods, as well as Swaledale tweed and supplies of wool. This is a very special place for real woollen knitwear using natural wool from British sheep, Swaledale, of course, and others such as Herdwick, Welsh or Wensleydale. There are no strident colours here for many items are in the undyed natural colours of the sheep, a range of cream, grey, light and dark browns, with only some blue, green or rust colour used to appeal to those who like a rather brighter design. Visitors will also find a very interesting display board which tells the story of sheep and demonstrates the uses of wool. What more useful reminder of a holiday could there be than a sweater knitted of Swaledale wool in the Dale itself?

There are no early records of potters in Swaledale but this is a craft which has become very popular in recent years and there are pottery workshops in the Dale and in Richmond. Their craftwork is displayed in local shops. Patchwork is another craft which has become popular in recent years and garments and other items in patchwork are also made locally.

The Dales have always inspired artists. A painting or a print, or a large photograph, of a scene makes a very pleasant reminder of a holiday, and visitors will find a large selection. People who fear that a painting will be too expensive may be surprised by the reasonable prices of many to be found locally. A print, drawn and made by the artist himself, will be less costly still. Interesting and unusual framed photographs are also worth looking for. Paintings, prints and photographs all give pleasure for many years to come.

It is possible to spend a pleasant day in Reeth, sitting on the wide green, eating delicious home-made ice-cream, and wandering round the small shops and galleries. The Reeth Gallery in Silver Street has on show local prints and paintings, pottery, locally made knitwear and the traditional hooked mats. There is a large choice here, with items to appeal to the taste of everyone. You are welcome to spend as much time as you like looking round, to choose that special memento of a holiday or to find unusual and fascinating items to take home for relatives or friends.

On many Sundays in summer, arts and craft fairs, some to raise money for a charity, are set up in the market hall in Richmond. Exhibitors at these do not necessarily come from the immediate local area and the craft work on display is not always the unique work of one artist. The range is wide and the visitor will find an attractive variety of stalls to choose from. Richmond, too, has many shops where locally made craft work can be found. At the Art Centre, it is possible to join a course and learn to draw or paint. The Centre also provides an outlet for local artists, and visitors will find paintings, pottery and printed silks on show, each article an individual piece of work by a real artist. It is situated on the Green, a delightful quiet triangle of grass surrounded by old houses.

A friend of Cromwell and the founder of a chapel and a Bible charity, it is easy to imagine Philip, Lord Wharton, as a strict puritanical figure. In fact, he was described as the handsomest young man in England and the greatest beau at the court of Charles I, particularly fond of dancing which showed off his fine legs. In spite of this, he became a staunch advocate of the Puritan cause, speaking on their behalf in the House of Lords. Although he supported the Parliament and fought on their side at the battle of Edgehill, he hoped for an agreement and did not approve of the king's execution. He subsequently refused all Cromwell's requests to take an active part in the government of the Commonwealth. In spite of this he remained a close friend of Cromwell and a marriage between his daughter and Cromwell's son Henry was discussed.

Wharton welcomed the return of Charles II. At the time he was in mourning for his wife's death, but to give his black clothes a look of joy had his buttons made of diamonds. His fine collection of pictures included the Van Dycks which are now in the Hermitage Museum in Leningrad. In 1689 he built the independent chapel at Smarber and he used the income from his lands at Healaugh to found a charity giving 1050 Bibles to non-conformist children who had learnt by heart seven psalms.

His son, Thomas Wharton, was an ardent supporter of the Whig party and he wrote a satirical poem about the Catholic king James II and Ireland. With the refrain 'Lilli burlero, bullen a la', mocking the Irish language, and set to music by Purcell, it became so immensely popular that Wharton used to say that he had sung a king out of three kingdoms. Wharton was the most astute party manager the Whigs ever had and one of the most successful politicians of his time, "He spared no expense, took a pride in making his constituents drunk on the best ale, and knew all the electors' children by name". He had a passion for horses, owned the best stud in the country, and said his greatest delight was in winning plates from tories and high-churchmen.

His n'er-do-well son Philip married at sixteen, became notorious as president of the Hell-fire Club, lost over £120,000 in the South Sea scheme, and declared himself a supporter of the Catholic Pretender James Stuart. He was eventually forced to leave England, all his estates being taken over by trustees.

The Whartons were among the first to develop the lead-mining extensively in Swaledale, encouraged by the success of the Bathurst operations in Arkengarthdale. John Bathurst was physician to Oliver Cromwell. His son and grandson were both Charles, and the C.B. Hotel carries their initials to this day.

Tryphosa Brockwell was born in Teesdale. As a young girl she married an actor from a strolling company but soon became more and more enamoured of acting and ambitious for the proper stage. Her third husband was Samuel Butler, originally a maker of stays in York, and she persuaded him to form a company to make a regular circuit of playhouses, which included Kendal, Whitby and Harrogate. Butler became a very successful manager and in 1788 built the theatre in Richmond, where he established a permanent home for the company and where Mrs Siddons, Edmund Kean, Macready and other famous actors came to perform.

On the wall of the old school in Muker are plaques commemorating Richard and Cherry Kearton. Their names may not be familiar to the younger generation but older people will remember the wild-life films made by Cherry Kearton before the last war. Born in Thwaite, where their birthplace can still be seen, they were pioneers of nature photography. Until then photographers had mainly used dead or stuffed animals but the Keartons spent patient hours in the wild and were able to produce books illustrated by photographs of wild life in a natural habitat.

The yeoman farmers of the Dales are seldom thought of as famous, yet they, perhaps more than any others, have made the Dales what they are. Typical were the Garths, who once lived at Crackpot. Farmers, masons and joiners, they expanded their activities over the years, improving their land and buying good stock. At the time of the Napoleonic Wars, their crops included oats and barley, turnips and potatoes. The family also acquired shares in the lead-mines and the coal-pit at Tan Hill. In 1862 they bought one of the first new patent mowing machines. Francis Garth began to breed a herd of pedigree Shorthorn cattle and was one of the founders of the Shorthorn Society in 1875. He built himself a new house, with a walled garden where apples, plums, pears, cherries and even a walnut tree were planted. Public affairs were not neglected. The Garths supported the church, attended political meetings, went to lectures on astronomy and chemistry and started a book club in Muker.

Marie Hartley and Joan Ingilby, who have made a unique record of the life and traditions of the Dales, lived in Swaledale for many years.

Legends and Romance

There is an old legend that King Arthur and his knights of the Round Table lie beneath the rock on which Richmond is built, asleep but ready to rise up should England find herself in peril. Arthur was probably the war-leader of a mobile force who fought the Saxon invaders in different places. Launcelot's castle of Joyous Gard may have been at either Bamburgh or Berwick-upon-Tweed and King Arthur has many associations with the North. A tale is told of how a certain Potter Thompson was exploring a cave beneath the rock and found himself in the chamber where the knights lie sleeping. Astonished, he could not resist putting out a hand to touch Excalibur. The sound of clanging armour and clashing swords immediately filled the air, the knights stirred and a voice called out, "Is it time?" Terrified for his life Potter Thompson fled from the chamber, and nobody was ever able to find the entrance again.

Another story tells of a mysterious passage beneath the obelisk in the market place. Once some soldiers put a drummer boy into the passage and told him to march along it beating his drum while they traced the route by following the sound outside. When they had got within half a mile of Easby Abbey, the sound suddenly stopped. The drummer boy was never seen again, though it is said that the sound of his drumming can still sometimes be heard.

"On Richmond Hill there lives a lass, More bright than May-day morn, Whose charms all other maids surpass, A rose without a thorn". The lass celebrated in this famous love-song was Frances l'Anson, whose family owned Hill House in Richmond. Written by her lover Leonard McNally, it was set to music by James Hook and sung first at Vauxhall in 1789, becoming immensely popular, and often wrongly appropriated by Richmond in Surrey. They had first met in London, but William l'Anson did not approve of McNally and he packed his daughter off to Yorkshire, not without reason, for McNally was an Irish lawyer of very dubious reputation, much disliked by his colleagues. McNally, however, came to Richmond where he succeeded in bribing a servant to help the lass escape. They were married in secret in London. Sadly her happiness was short-lived, for she died in child-birth a few years later.

The artist Turner has put the lass into the foreground of his paintings of Richmond. In one watercolour she can be seen playing with her dog; in another she is carrying a milking stool while two dogs follow behind; in yet another she is teaching her dog to stand on its hind legs.

Commissioned to make a series of pictures to serve as illustrations to a projected history of the County of York, but never completed, Turner embarked on a comprehensive tour. It was his habit to make numerous line drawings as he travelled, small but very accurate as to the shapes of trees, waterfalls, buildings or windows. Such was the small sketch he made of Marrick Priory, to be later turned into a watercolour with the romantic priory tower, grown somewhat in height, standing against a background of misty distant hills. Turner's atmospheric paintings allow for "A certain enlargement of scale due to remembrance of effect", as one commentator put it.

Romance is made to suit our time, too. The popular novels by Barbara Taylor Bradford "A Woman of Substance" and "Hold the Dream" tell the story of Emma Harte, a Yorkshire lass, penniless and abandoned by her lover, who goes to America and builds a successful business empire. She achieves wealth and luxury, but her roots and her heart remain in Yorkshire. Some of the outdoor scenes of the enjoyable TV series of these books were shot in Richmond and in Arkengarthdale. The house where her mother lived was in Langthwaite and the scenes of Emma's own funeral were filmed there.

The most famous TV series of all associated with this area is, of course, "All Creatures Great and Small". James Herriot is the pseudonym for a real vet who did live and work in Yorkshire, and it was only in his fifties that he began to write down his experiences. To many people, alongside the humour of the tales, they present an ideal countryside, full of 'characters', happy in their lives in village and farm, very different from the fast-paced stress of real life, and where every potential disaster reassuringly turns out all right in the end. Arkengarthdale features also in this TV series. The small rustic pub, the Red Lion, in Langthwaite has provided a background for some episodes. The water-splash is on the moorland road between Arkengarthdale and Low Row and the small bridge over which the vets' car drives is over the Arkle Beck in Langthwaite, both very familiar to viewers. In addition, the set used for scenes in the vets' surgery can be seen now in the Richmondshire Museum in Richmond.

One real character of whom tales are told was Neddy Dick, who lived at Keld. He realised that different pieces of stone, when struck, produce different notes of music and he eventually collected a complete scale. Sadly his 'rock music' was lost when he died.

Detailed opening times of museums and historic sites are not given here as these vary with the season. Visitors who have an interest in one particular place are advised to check opening times before making a special journey.

INTEREST AND ACTIVITY IN RICHMOND

RICHMOND Dominated by its huge castle, the town is well worth exploring on foot, with its huge cobbled market place, old narrow wynds dating from medieval times, and wide streets of Georgian houses. The C18th was a time of prosperity, and much of the town built then has survived remarkably unaltered to the present day. A town trail with a map is available from the Tourist Office. Market day is on Saturday with a multitude of outdoor stalls. There is also a mini-indoor market on Thursday. Early closing, Wednesday. For car parking, see 'Useful Information'. See also section, 'Eighteenth Century Elegance'.

RICHMOND CASTLE This was one of the first castles to be built in stone, and it also contains Scollands Hall, a remarkable early domestic building with a hall and solar on the first floor. The great keep was added in 1160 and is rivalled only by London and Rochester. Constructed originally to defend the Normans against the conquered English, the need for such a fortification gradually disappeared as the country became more peaceful. The castle never became the residence of an important family, as did Raby, and was gradually allowed to fall into dilapidation, most of it being roofless by the C16th. The view from the top is magnificent and a visit to this impressive medieval fortress is usually much enjoyed by children. It is open daily. See also 'Stone Castle and Norman Forest'.

EASBY ABBEY These interesting monastic ruins lie about a mile east of Richmond and can be reached either by car or by a pleasant walk which starts near the swimming pool and winds its way between the river and high wooded banks. The gatehouse and the frater are the best preserved remains and give some idea of past magnificence. Originally founded in 1151 for 13 monks, the abbey accumulated gifts of land and much wealth, although it had only 18 monks at the Dissolution. The artist Turner painted a picture of the ruined abbey, properly called St. Agatha's. The ruins are open daily. Car park. See also 'Monks, Nuns and Friars'.

GREYFRIARS TOWER This beautiful tower, in colourful gardens, is all that survives of the friary which once stood outside the walls of the medieval town. Friars Wynd, a narrow alley, once led to it through the small arched gateway which still survives. See also 'Monks, Nuns and Friars'.

GEORGIAN THEATRE ROYAL This theatre was built in 1788 and, although put to other uses for many years until recently, has fortunately survived as a unique example of a Georgian playhouse. Performances are given regularly. It is possible to make a fascinating guided tour of the auditorium, stage and dressing rooms, and to visit the museum which contains remarkable painted scenery of 1836 and also various stage mementoes. It is open in the afternoons from May to September.

GREEN HOWARDS MUSEUM This museum, beautifully set out, displays the history, medals, silver and relics of this famous North Yorkshire Regiment. There is a magnificent display of their red uniforms, and of that of some local volunteer battalions, up to the less glamorous though more practical clothing of today. Also on display is a fine collection of Richmond's civic plate. The museum is open daily in summer, on weekdays out of season, but closed in January and December.

RICHMONDSHIRE MUSEUM The history of Richmond is told here with mementoes of the past, tools and machinery of former days and photographs of early bicycling days and Richmond Meet. Displays include costumes and a remarkable collection of needlework necessities. The museum is open from Easter to October in the afternoons, and also some mornings.

THE FALLS In a beautiful setting below the walls of the castle, the river drops over flat rocks in a series of waterfalls and pools, where hardy people play in the water. It is very popular with older children. Advance flood warnings, however, should never be ignored. There is a car park with toilets.

HUDSWELL NATIONAL TRUST PROPERTY South of the river, Billy Banks Wood, Round Howe and Hag Wood, 39 hectares (94 acres), can be reached by a path from Richmond Bridge, where there is a car park. This mixed woodland is on a north-facing slope and is at its best on a bright day.

RICHMONDSHIRE SWIMMING POOL This is a modern indoor pool, with separate teaching pool, built to an award-winning design and glass-enclosed so that the trees outside are visible. There is a bar and cafeteria. It is open daily although times vary slightly.

INTEREST AND ACTIVITY IN THE DALES

REETH Formerly a much more important place, Reeth has attractive and varied buildings round an exceptionally large green, with plenty of space to park. With views of the surrounding hills, it is a very pleasant place to sit, where one can enjoy delicious home-made ice-cream, a speciality of Reeth, or look round a craft workshop, art gallery or gift shop. Early closing is on Thursday but in summer and at popular holiday times visitors will find that many places remain open all day and are also open on Sundays. Reeth has an interesting variety of buildings from the C18th and C19th, and is also the home of the Swaledale Folk Museum. See also 'Eighteenth Century Elegance' -final part.

SWALEDALE FOLK MUSEUM This is the place to go if you want to understand the landscape and the villages of the Dale. Here the visitor can learn, with well set out and clearly captioned displays, how the stone houses were built, what implements the farmers used, what life was like for girls who entered domestic service, often their only option. Visitors who intend to visit some of the lead-mining remains in the Dale will find it much easier to understand the workings of the hushes, levels and ruined buildings if they have previously looked at the display in the museum with its clear explanations and diagrams and the tools used by the miners. The museum is open daily from April to the end of October.

GUNNERSIDE GILL LEAD MINING REMAINS It is possible to do a circular walk of about 5 miles (8 kilometres), which leads past the extensive remains of the lead mining activity of former days, with an explanatory leaflet produced by the National Park Authority and available in local shops. Starting in the village of Gunnerside the leaflet directs the walker up the Gill past spoil heaps, hushes, mine entrances and the remains of various buildings, with brief explanations of their former use.

There are numerous remains of the lead mining in other parts of Swaledale and Arkengarthdale and the National Park Authority has made agreements with the owners of three smelt mills; Surrender, Old Gang and Grinton, which will enable these interesting relics of a former industry to be preserved and repaired. It must be emphasized that no attempt to enter any of the old mines should be made as they are now very unstable, in many cases flooded, and extremely dangerous.

WATERFALLS The steep-sided valley of Swaledale has many waterfalls but the most spectacular and the most famous are at the head of the Dale near Keld. **Wainwath Force**, where the river drops over wide steps, is close to the B6270 road. The surrounding land is private but the National Park Authority has arranged access for visitors. **Kisdon Force** and **East Gill Force** are reached by a short walk from the small square in Keld village (note that parking here is severely restricted and cars may be better left on the road above the village). East Gill Force is close to a foot-bridge where a side stream joins the main river. Kisdon Force, in a spectacular gorge, is on the Swale itself.

THE BUTTERTUBS These curious limestone formations, the result of the rock dissolving in water, are on high ground between Thwaite and Hawes (in Wensleydale). The origin of the name is obscure. Some think that they are so called because the fluted sides resemble old butter tubs, while others say that farmers used to lower butter into their depths to keep cool if it could not be sold immediately at market!

WHITCLIFFE SCAR AND WOODS On the old road between Marske and Richmond, this is a popular place for a stroll or easy ramble, with some beautiful views over the Dale. **Beacon Hill**, by this same road, is a remarkable viewpoint, from which the towers of York Minster, some 40 miles away, can been seen on a clear day.

WALKS Because Swaledale in the past was such a busy place, with miners going to work, pack-horses and drovers, numerous footpaths spread out from the villages. Keld, Muker, Thwaite, Gunnerside, Reeth, Grinton and Langthwaite are all good starting places. For those who prefer to devise their own route, the Ordnance Survey Outdoor Leisure Map 30, The 'Yorkshire Dales Northern Area', shows footpaths very clearly. Maps and booklets of suggested walks are available in local shops. The National Park Authority publishes some descriptive leaflets, and visitors are also invited to join walks conducted by a local warden.

PICNIC PLACES Officially designated sites: **The Batts, Richmond**, near the old station, with picnic tables and seats. **Round Howe, Richmond**, signposted on the B6270 road to Reeth, with picnic tables and seats. There are many other places where people can draw in a car by the side of the road. Please be careful not to obstruct any entrances, and remember that although moorland is not fenced, this does not mean that the public has a right of access.

THE LOWER DALE

DOWNHOLME From the Anglian 'dun' (a hill), this village was in existence at the time of the Domesday Book, and there are traces of strip lynchets (old ploughed fields) nearby. The church is a Norman foundation. Not far away is the privately owned Walburn Hall, an imposing fortified manor house, built as a defence against sporadic Scots raids. In the Civil War it was a royalist stronghold.

ELLERTON Only a ruined tower, on private ground, remains of this Cistercian nunnery, one of the smallest in England. It probably never had more than 13 nuns and by the time of the Dissolution only five.

FREMINGTON An Anglian name. There was once a corn mill here, using water from the river to drive the mill-wheel. Thomas Elliot of Fremington was one of the prime advocates of enclosure of land in the C18th.

GRINTON An Anglian name. At one time one of the largest parishes in the country, the church here was the only one in the Dale and all corpses had to be brought here for burial along a route known as the Corpse Way. This fine building dates mainly from the C15th though some Norman work still remains. Because people lived at great distances, a fair was allowed here on Sundays.

HUDSWELL Recorded in the Domesday Book, this was later a stopping place for pack-horse traders coming from Lancaster and at that time was a busy place with a number of inns.

HURST On moorland north of Marrick, it was formerly a busy lead-mining village, and the remains of this activity are very evident in the surrounding countryside. There is a tradition that the Romans mined lead here.

MARRICK The old road from Richmond to Reeth, came past here so it was formerly a much more important place. A number of paths still radiate from the village. It had no church and the paved path and 375 steps, known as 'The Nuns' Causey', which lead down to Marrick Priory, may have been built primarily to enable the villagers to reach the Priory church. The fields to the north of Marrick illustrate the geometric regularity of the enclosures of the late C18th.

MARRICK PRIORY A Benedictine Nunnery founded in 1154, the nuns received grants of land and kept 80 cows, 500 ewes, horses and pigs, being permitted to employ secular workers as labourers. There were a prioress and 16 nuns at the time of the Dissolution in 1540. Today it is a private educational and training centre associated with the diocese of Ripon.

MARSKE This attractive village set in woodland has a Norman church which was restored in the C17th. Marske Hall, now private flats, was one of the earliest houses built by John Carr of York in the Palladian style of the 1750s, with classical pillared doorway and symmetrical frontage. It was the home of the Hutton family and the obelisk which is a notable feature in the landscape is a memorial to Captain Matthew Hutton, who desired to be buried in a place from which he had often admired the view.

WHITCLIFFE SCAR Inscribed stones here celebrate the remarkable escape from death of Robert Willance in 1606. While out hunting and suddenly enveloped in fog, his horse plunged over the precipice. The horse was killed but Willance escaped with only a broken leg. He placed the stones here in gratitude for his providential escape.

REETH AND THE UPPER DALE

REETH Reeth was originally an Anglian village recorded in the Domesday Book as Rie. It is by the Arkle Beck and the name is derived from the Anglo-Saxon word for a stream. A typical Anglian village clustered round an open space into which cattle could be driven at night for safety, and the present village lies round a large green, nowadays quiet in winter but in summer full of people enjoying the wide space in its beautiful setting. To the west of the village, the grassed over lines of old Anglian ploughed fields can still be seen. In an advantageous position where Arkengarthdale joins the main valley of the Swale, it became an important market centre, as the large cobbled market place still shows, its charter dating from 1695. The C18th and the early C19th were times of prosperity when many of the houses were built or rebuilt, and also places of worship, schools and institutes, as well as hotels for the needs of traders and visitors. There is no Anglican church as it is in the parish of Grinton. The interesting Swaledale Folk Museum occupies a former Methodist Sunday School. By the end of the C19th, with declining prosperity and loss of population, the weekly market was discontinued, but Reeth still has its annual agricultural show in September. Today in summer the wide green and a variety of craft shops attract large numbers of visitors.

GUNNERSIDE Its name comes from a Norse owner, Gunnar. The small fields close to the village are remarkable surviving examples of early C16th enclosures. At one time a centre of lead-mining in the Dale, the houses built to accommodate the mining community crowd close together. There is a very fine Methodist chapel. The village is at the foot of Gunnerside Gill and a path up the Gill goes through a dramatic gorge to the extensive remains of the lead-mining industry.

HEALAUGH The name means 'a clearing in the forest' and suggests that it was an Anglian settlement founded as the population of the earlier villages expanded. In later years the manor of Healaugh was the largest in the Dale and at one time the property of the Wharton family. Healaugh was a centre of Quaker worship and Quakers here maintained their faith after it had declined elsewhere.

IVELET the beautiful single arch bridge was originally built for pack-horses. It is supposed to be haunted by a headless dog.

KELD A Norse name meaning 'a spring'. The village is built around a small square and is today astride the Pennine Way and the Coast to Coast Walk and is also a starting point for walks down Kisdon Gorge or to admire the many waterfalls. Houses here and in nearby Angram are built in a particularly fine and closely grained stone which was taken from many small quarries in the local area.

LOW ROW AND FEETHAM Now one long village, many houses were built for miners. There are beautiful views of meadows and barns from the edge of the green. Thomas Armstrong, famous for his novel 'The Crowthers of Brankdam', lived here. In 1952 he published 'Adam Brunskill', in which life in the lead mines of former days is most realistically recreated.

MUKER Its name derived from a Norse word meaning 'a narrow field'. The village is built alongside the Muker Beck, close to where it joins the Swale. When a church was built here in 1580, it was no longer necessary to carry corpses to Grinton. Muker still has a Silver Band, carrying on a once popular Dales tradition, and an annual agricultural show. There is a National Park Information Point in the village store, which has a tea shop. At nearby Usha Gap is a farm site for camping and caravans.

THWAITE Another Norse name, meaning 'a clearing in woodland'. This small village was the birthplace of Richard and Cherry Kearton, pioneers in wild-life photography, and today a delightful stone lintel carved with birds and animals marks their home.

ARKENGARTHDALE

ARKLE TOWN About the year 1100 AD, Count Alan Rufus of Richmond put Robert Arkhil in charge of this area, then to be kept as forest for hunting. From him the Arkle Beck and Arkengarthdale get their names. It was in Arkle Town that the first church was built in 1145. Sadly it was later allowed to deteriorate so much that it was demolished in 1818.

BOOZE Not what it seems, but meaning 'a house by a curve'. This area was once the centre of a huge lead-mining industry, and at one time there were 41 miners houses here.

ESKELETH One of the great drove roads from Scotland came down Arkengarthdale from Dale Head to a ford at Eskeleth, and this remote place saw the passage of thousands of cattle on their way from the Highlands of Scotland to the industrial towns of England. Motorists, note that the minor road by High Eskeleth is steep, gated and extremely narrow.

LANGTHWAITE This small village of grey stone is now familiar to millions as a setting for the first 'Herriot' series on TV, when the vets' car was seen driving over the bridge. The fine Methodist chapel is a reminder of the days when Langthwaite was full of lead miners, devoted to the teachings of Wesley. Opposite is the Anglican church built in 1817 after years of neglect. The CB hotel commemorates Charles Bathhurst, whose family did so much to develop the lead-mining industry in Arkengarthdale.

WHAW Written as 'Le Kauwhe' in 1285, it meant 'an enclosure for cows'. Although the Dale was reserved for hunting, some farming was allowed. Sheep, formerly kept by the Norse farmers, were forbidden, but cows, more easily kept on limited pastures, were permitted to graze in certain places for part of the year.

TAN HILL This remote inn, at 528 metres (1732 ft.) above sea level the highest in England, was once the crossing point of important pack-horse trails, and crowded with travellers. Because of the coal pits nearby, an early turnpike road was made to Tan Hill through Arkengarthdale. But the invention of rail transport put an end to pack-horses and cattle-droving and the inn lost its custom. An important sheep sale is still held here.